CW01496224

Revitalizing Christianity: The Theology of Peter Lewis.

A Collection of Short Articles edited by Shane St Reynolds

Foreword by the Honourable Michael Kirby AC CMG

DEDICATION

This compilation of articles is dedicated to the courageous folk who dare to question, to seek, and to journey. May these pages serve as a beacon of light, guiding you towards a richer, more profound understanding of faith and a more compassionate way of living.

TERMS/ABBREVIATIONS

LGBT+

The term LGBT+ includes a wide range of sexual orientations and gender identities, including Lesbian, Gay, Bisexual, and Transgender; the plus sign represents other identities such as Intersex, Queer or Questioning, Asexual, and others, used to describe the diversity of LGBT+ folk and acknowledge the wide range of human experiences and identities that fall under this umbrella term.

Progressive Christianity

A spiritually open, enquiring path of engagement with the Christian tradition and the life and teachings of Jesus. By calling ourselves progressive Christians, we mean we are Christians who believe that following Jesus' teachings can lead to a deeper awareness of the Sacred and the unity of all life, recognizing these teachings as one of many paths to this understanding, and we value wisdom from diverse sources; we seek an inclusive community for all people regardless of belief, identity, or background; we understand that our actions reflect our beliefs; we value questioning over absolutes in our pursuit of understanding; we are dedicated to promoting peace, justice, environmental stewardship, and a lifelong commitment to learning, compassion, and selfless love.

SUSTAINABILITY STATEMENT

Having already published several books, I feel that this new publication represents a fresh chapter in my journey. When I first submitted the manuscript to a mainstream publisher, I was disheartened to learn that their pricing would place the book in the $30-$40 range. This didn't align with my goal of sharing this Christian message widely and affordably.

So, I decided to take a different route. As an experienced author, I chose to self-publish through Amazon KDP. This decision allows me to offer the book at a much lower price, making it accessible to many more readers. By managing the marketing myself, I can ensure that the message reaches those who need it without causing financial strain.

My commitment goes beyond just affordability. I am also passionate about environmental stewardship. By using Amazon's print-on-demand technology, I am helping to reduce waste and lower the ecological impact associated with traditional publishing methods, including its carbon footprint. This aligns with the biblical mandate found in Genesis 2:15 where it says, "The Lord God took the man and put him in the Garden of Eden to work it and take care of it."

I also strive to be socially responsible. Keeping the price low enables the book to reach a broader audience, staying true to my mission of spreading the message rather than focusing on profit. This approach allows me to uphold my values and maintain transparency throughout the book's production and distribution. It is important for me to adhere to high ethical standards and ensure that every aspect of this project reflects the principles that guide me.

Thank you for joining us on this journey.

FOREWORD

THE HONOURABLE MICHAEL KIRBY AC CMG

The Hon. Michael Kirby was born in Sydney, Australia, where he also received his education in public schools. Following his career as a solicitor and barrister, he was appointed to the judiciary in 1975. Kirby served in several prominent courts, including as President of the Court of Appeal of NSW and as a Justice of the High Court of Australia. He has held various roles with the United Nations and other international organizations. Additionally, he occasionally attends services at St James's Anglican Church on King Street in Sydney, which recently celebrated its 200th anniversary and extends a warm welcome to all attendees.

Like me, Shane St Reynolds identifies as a Christian, following the tradition of Protestant Anglicanism. In my case, I do this because this was the tradition in which my parents were raised and raised me. I have never changed. This is a fairly typical story of the current age.

For a long time, I simply accepted what I was taught about religion, without too much doubt or questioning. This was certainly the case when I was very young. Every week I would attend the Sunday School for Church of England children of the parish. We sat in the pews of St Andrew's Church on the corner of Parramatta Road and Concord Road in the Sydney Diocese of Anglicanism. As I grew older, at my schools in Sydney, I participated in the single period of the week named "Scripture". This was a weekly interval of 40 minutes when a visiting clergyman would be allowed on to the sternly secular school grounds to present a lesson for school children who opted to attend. Because my schooling was exclusively in schools provided by the State of New South Wales Department of Education, they were controlled by the language of the local legislature. They were committed to a trinity of principles. These were that education would be "free, secular and compulsory".

In my experience, this trinity was quite faithfully observed in my experience. Attending the "scripture class" was not, as such, compulsory. A special room was set aside in my high school for "non-scripture". This provided supervision; but no instruction in secular ethics that later became available. It comprised children at the school who did not identify with any of the mostly Protestant religious denominations of that time: Church of England; Methodist; Presbyterian, Congregationalist; and Baptist. Most of the school children in those days, in the early 1950s, aligned with Church of England (as the Anglicans were then named). This was far the biggest group. We convened in the School Hall. It was rumoured that a small cohort of our fellow students were Jewish, who attended "non-scripture". There were also some Roman Catholics amongst the school students. They, or more likely their parents, had opted out of the separate system of Catholic parochial schools. Most children of that religion were isolated from the corrupting influence of the questioning Protestants. There may have been some Pentecostal students. Perhaps there were even some Plymouth Brethren or Jehovah Witness students. If so, they probably elected to join the most congenial tradition for their beliefs (presumably Baptist).

As the annual census of the Australian population showed, in those days, the Church of England was by far the biggest Christian cohort of the population. They represented about 40% of the population. Catholicism constituted about 20%. There was a tiny fraction of Jewish believers. There were also, it was darkly rumoured, some lost souls amongst the students who had no religious belief. That seemed quite extraordinary to me at the time. How could they have survived without receiving the "truth" of Christianity. A religion built on the life and instruction of Jesus of Nazareth, the Son of God.

Looking back on those days, I can see that secularism was strongly infused in the values I was taught. They were civil values. They included to respect and serve the King (King George VI), soon, in 1952, to be replaced by Queen Elizabeth II. They included to defend our basic social institutions, including parliaments elected by regular, compulsory voting. And courts operating in the city and in local suburbs. The public service which was independent and uncorrupted. And public schools without "bells and smells" served at least 70% of the school aged population.

There were very few people of colour in our neighbourhoods, shopping centres; and schools in those days. I do not believe that there were any Islamic students at any of the schools that I attended. No Hindus. No Buddhists. No Sikhs. No Jains. No other faiths to cast doubts to young minds about the universality and truth of Christian beliefs.

There were features of my childhood religious experience that greatly attracted me.

The fact that it was a Reformed (Protestant) tradition, exhibiting features of rationality and Christian simplicity;

* It resisted non-Biblical designation of a church officeholder gifted with powers of infallibility in matters theological;

* It rejected dogmas that had no adequate foundation in scripture (including the virtual deification of Mary, Jesus's mother);

* It generally disdained medieval traditions such as the Roman Catholic use of incense and candles; denial of marriage to clergy; denial of access to wine in the sacrament of communion; belief in transubstantiation and other non-Biblical teachings;

* The affirmative simplicity of church decoration, especially the simple, bare altar with its empty cross, to symbolise not the dead Saviour but the Risen Lord; and;

* Emphasis on the life and teaching of Jesus as portrayed in the Gospel story. This seemed closer to the essential Christianity that I was taught, rather than other more extravagant, worldly and power conscious denominations of the Christian religion.

These elements in my Protestant upbringing appear to be, in some ways, similar to those propounded by Dr Peter Lewis. Also, by his predecessor, Bishop John Shelby Spong (of New Jersey); and his admirer Shane St Reynolds (of Australia). Although for many decades, I repeated mechanically the apostles' Creed and never paused to question the recited components of the Christian credo, it was easier for me, as it earlier appeared to Bishop Spong, Dr Peter Lewis, and Mr Shane St Reynolds, to question so called "core beliefs" than it might have been for a Christian of inerrant Catholic or fundamentalist opinions or of medieval traditions.

One by one, I came to question and ultimately to doubt many elements in the Creed, just as Dr Peter Lewis does in his essays, published in this text. When I familiarised myself with Dr Peter Lewis's approach, especially as expounded by Shane St Reynolds, I immediately recognised the attractions of "Progressive Christianity", as explained in this book. Like Peter and Shane, but by my own reasoning, I came to conclusions similar to those outlined in this text:

*   Rejecting doctrines of original sin, and the belief that human sexuality is inherently sinful;

*   Seriously doubting the resurrection of the body and life everlasting;

*   Rejecting parts of the Bible said to be inerrant, although resulting in the beliefs manifestly incompatible with contemporary values, knowledge, and scientific research;

*   Contesting the notion of Jesus's "virgin birth"; and

*   Accepting the human and also the divine features of Jesus as features essential to his message.

The possibility that the inclusive and universal character of Jesus would sustain a belief that He would have been indifferent to same-sex attraction on the part of disciples or of anyone else – or even of Himself – does not necessarily require the presupposition that Jesus was Himself same-sex attracted. There would have been many historical features of the times in which He lived, that would have made even thinking about such a subject especially unlikely. On the other hand, drawing upon earlier writers on "Progressive Christianity", Peter and Shane have raised the hypothesis that, in today's terms, Jesus may Himself have been homosexual or 'gay'. His gentle, loving nature, as described in Scripture, would fit comfortably with such a characteristic. Assigning Him to a minority characteristic of humanity is not essential for an appreciation of His loving nature. It lies at the core of His being, as explained in Scripture. In this sense, the character of Jesus as described in Scripture, is quite different from a masculinist characteristic of the heroes of the Jewish Talmud (Moses, Isaiah and Solomon); the Prophet Muhammad (of Islamic belief); or of Guru Nanak (of Sikhism). Growing up with a realisation of my own sexuality as 'gay' was not as great a burden for me as a Christian as it would have been if my parents had imbued me with religious beliefs of other and different faiths. The presence of Jesus in my life was comforting, reassuring, approachable and loving.

As the Progressive Christian theology of Peter Lewis and Shane St Reynolds demonstrate in these pages, when immaterial features of traditional Christian beliefs are cut away, the core elements of a Christian faith narrow themselves down to a relatively small number of essential beliefs, deriving from the recorded instruction of Jesus to His followers on how they should interrelate with each other and the world. One of those core elements is the instruction to love one another; to forgive those who do one wrong; and to love a single deity in accordance with a new Covenant. This new Covenant was more loving, kindly, forgiving and empathetic than the old Covenant of the Jews; or of other religious beliefs, growing up elsewhere in different social and physical circumstances.

It was this "essence" of Christianity that I saw in my youth as a redeeming feature of Jesus-based religion. I believe that it also helps Peter Lewis and Shane St Reynolds to explore the possibilities of Progressive Christianity. It explains the attractions of a more modern and less superstitious attraction of the Modern Christianity that is explained in this book.

No one approaching these pages will immediately embrace everything that the authors, Peter and Shane, have propounded. Their 'theology', if such it is, is work in progress. It is part of the continuing advances that are needed, assigning His empathy and forgiveness for those viewed as different (Samaritans) or immoral ('cast the first stone'), to reconcile traditional Faith and scriptural texts with the rational worlds of Copernicus, Charles Darwin, Alfred Kinsey, and other scientists who explain the universe and the world we live in.

This is why many, who like me, have been raised in Christian beliefs, often come to a fork in the road. As they are reciting the Apostles' Creed, they will stumble over declarations of faith written in earlier superstitious simpler, and pre-scientific times. When they reach that point, many will throw away altogether the spiritual beliefs in which they had been raised. They will reject troublesome disharmony between their traditional Faith of their fathers and the scientific world of today. Or they will yearn for a third approach that rejects the superstition but clings on to the core beliefs that bound them in love to their families and to their earliest spiritual experiences.

It is this third pathway that Dr Peter Lewis and his acolyte, Shane St Reynolds, have taken. As one who is also on the path they have trodden before, I thank them for their reflections. Those reflections will by no means attract a new post Lutheran Reformation. The times today are different. However, they may help many to search for the core reasons for human existence and how we, who still accept the essential loving messages of Jesus, can like Peter and Shane, find a new Progressive Christianity. A religion that acknowledges Jesus as human, yet divine.

Others will denounce the views of Progressive Christians as heretical and impertinent. Yet simply demanding that Christian and other believers of Orthodox religions should accept, unquestioning, ancient Credos of the past, unchanged, is much less possible and less acceptable than it was in days gone by. Progressive Christians will increasingly face rejection by the orthodox and search for new beliefs that reconcile the old religion with current times and fresh realities. We may be banished from our Faith by others who are proudly dogmatic, inflexible and strictly textual in their convictions. However, Jesus Himself questioned the beliefs of His own times. When we do so today, we are being faithful to the New Covenant that Jesus proclaimed.

1 October 2024   Michael Kirby

x

CONTENTS

INTRODUCTION

Have you ever felt your faith could use a refresh? Dr. Peter Lewis, a prominent figure in progressive Christianity, offers a transformative perspective on Christian thought that both challenges traditional viewpoints and deepens your connection with Jesus. This collection, "Revitalizing Christianity: The Theology of Peter Lewis," explores his profound insights, making them accessible to both seasoned believers and those in search of a fresh outlook. Through a series of thought-provoking articles and critiques, this book aims to guide you on a journey of exploration, helping you contribute your unique perspective to the ongoing faith conversation.

Beyond being a notable theologian, Peter is a cherished friend who has become a leading voice in progressive Christianity. His impactful work reaches a diverse audience, including academics and laypeople, through platforms such as Anglican Focus, Cccrh.org, UC Forum, and Progressivechristianity.org.

After a distinguished surgical career, Peter has dedicated his later years to evangelism, infusing his writings with a deep devotion. His works, such as *"The Ending of Mark's Gospel"* and *"Susan's Faith"* showcase both his theological depth and imaginative power.

This collection serves as a window to Peter's insightful approach to Christian thought. Beyond the ideas explored here, his published works demonstrate a remarkable ability to blend intellectual rigor with captivating storytelling. Take, for example, *"The Ending of Mark's Gospel"* where Peter applies a forensic lens to this debated scripture, illuminating its impact on our understanding of the Gospels and Christianity. In contrast, *"Susan's Faith"* utilizes a captivating narrative to explore theological issues through a personal faith journey of the character Susan, prompting readers to engage with their own beliefs.

The articles presented in this collection showcase Peter's intellectual curiosity and commitment to exploring Christian theology. He tackles challenging topics like reinterpreting Jesus, the nature of God, and the suffering servant in Isaiah. His fresh perspectives challenge traditional views, invigorate thought, and inspire.

In true Peter Lewis fashion, these articles don't shy away from difficult questions. Instead, they encourage readers to engage critically with scripture and theology, fostering a deeper and more personal understanding of faith.

It is my hope that this collection serves not only as a tribute to Peter's scholarship but also as a catalyst for ongoing dialogue and exploration within the realm of progressive Christian theology. As readers engage with Peter's insights and thought-provoking reflections, may they find inspiration to delve deeper into the rich tapestry of Christian thought, and may they be empowered to contribute their own unique perspectives to the ongoing conversation.

Marcella Althaus-Reid observed, marginalized theologies often struggle for acceptance by the mainstream, yet it is precisely at the margins that we might encounter a truer sense of the divine. If we deconstruct conventional ideas, we may discover that God is not what we initially expect. I hope these articles inspire new ideas, deepen faith, and encourage thoughtful reimagining and questioning.

As editor, I've taken the liberty to include critiques of each of Peter's articles at the end of their respective chapters, recognizing that questioning is an important part of our faith. Peter's work actively encourages such exploration. These critiques provide reflective insights, examining the strengths, weaknesses, and implications of Peter's arguments.

On a personal level, Peter's friendship has been a constant source of guidance throughout my journey of faith, which has been anything but smooth for someone navigating diverse beliefs. His support has not only brightened my academic pursuits but also nurtured my spiritual growth, especially during uncertain times. Understanding Jesus academically is one thing, but experiencing a deep, personal connection with Him goes far beyond scholarly study. Having a friend like Peter to journey with has truly made all the difference.

From the initial spark of my writing endeavours to the foreword Peter wrote for my book *'Faith & Sexuality: Reconciling LGBT+ People and Christianity'* Peter's friendship has been a source of strength. As Proverbs 27:17 reminds us, 'As iron sharpens iron, so one person sharpens another.'

In the spirit of Peter's approach, echoing the parable of new wineskins found in Mark 2:22, this collection is offered as a fresh vessel for these progressive theological ideas. Just as fermenting wine demands new wineskins, fresh perspectives are required to grapple with the complexities of our evolving faith. As you engage with Peter's insights, may they challenge your existing frameworks and inspire you to embrace the ongoing conversation. With Peter as our guide, let us embark on a journey of discovery and rediscovery, revitalizing Christianity for generations to come.

With every blessing,

Shane St Reynolds (GDTheol)
Author & Editor
TheGoodNewsBlog.org

CELESTIAL CAPTAIN

VISIO DIVINA

Before we begin, let's explore the concept of Visio Divina, or "divine seeing." This practice encourages a deep, contemplative engagement with visual imagery. In his essay "Meditation in a Toolshed[1]," C.S. Lewis describes a moment when he observed a beam of sunlight streaming through a crack in a dark toolshed. At first, this beam, filled with floating dust particles, seemed to dominate his view. However, when he shifted his perspective, the beam vanished, revealing a broader scene of green leaves moving on a tree outside and, beyond that, the distant sun. This experience highlights the difference between looking at something and looking along it—transitioning from a narrow focus to a deeper, more expansive understanding.

Visio Divina is a practice that involves viewing an image with intention and openness, allowing it to speak to your heart and spirit. As you move through this book, I encourage you to take a moment with each image, letting it guide your thoughts and reflections. This practice of visual meditation complements the written word, creating

---

[1] Originally published in The Coventry Evening Telegraph on July 17, 1945, and later reprinted in God in the Dock (Eerdmans, 1970; pages 212-15)

a holistic approach to exploring the themes and insights presented in each chapter.

By engaging with these images, you open yourself to a more profound spiritual experience, allowing the divine to reach you through both sight and thought. Embrace this visual divine practice as a way to enhance your journey through the book, making each chapter not just a reading experience but a meditative encounter with the sacred.

Steps for Practicing Visio Divina:

1. **Prepare**: Find a quiet space where you can focus without distractions. Take a few deep breaths to centre yourself.
2. **Gaze**: Look at the image with soft eyes, allowing it to capture your attention. Notice the details, colours, and shapes.
3. **Reflect**: Consider what emotions or thoughts the image evokes. How does it resonate with your current state of mind or spiritual journey?
4. **Pray**: Offer a prayer or hold a moment of silence, inviting the divine to speak to you through the image.
5. **Meditate**: Spend a few minutes in meditation, letting the image guide your reflections and insights.
6. **Respond**: Write down any thoughts, feelings, or inspirations that arise from your engagement with the image.

By following these steps, you'll deepen your spiritual connection and enrich your understanding of the divine as you explore this book. Imagine it as a journey akin to Captain Jean-Luc Picard's mission on the Enterprise, where each discovery brings greater insight and light. Approach each image with prayerful openness, allowing it to draw you closer to God. Just as Picard's crew seeks new truths, let these images illuminate your path, enhancing your faith and spiritual journey.

A REBEL IN NAZARETH

1 JESUS WAS DIFFERENT
BY DR. PETER E. LEWIS PUBLISHED ON: APRIL 30, 2021

Since writing the 2nd edition of my book *The Ending of Mark's Gospel: The Key to Understanding the Gospels and Christianity* in 2020 I have come to realize how different Jesus was and that his life before his baptism was the foundation for what became Christianity. Although his mission began suddenly when he was about 30, his previous experience must have provided the motivation for what he said and did.

According to Mark, Jesus's birth was natural, but he was very different from everyone around him, and he knew it. His relatives thought he was mad (Mark 3:21) and went to take charge of him. They knew he was different, and the most likely reason for this was that he was illegitimate, the result of his mother being raped by a Roman soldier when Sepphoris, just a few kilometres from Nazareth, was sacked by Roman forces after the death of King Herod in 4 BC. So, Jesus looked different, probably with non-Jewish features.

He was also different in other ways. He was obviously very intelligent and religiously minded, and as a carpenter he would have been involved in the rebuilding of Sepphoris, which was the capital of

1

Galilee and a centre of Jewish culture. It was probably there, rather than in his village of Nazareth, that he learnt the Hebrew scriptures, and in the gospels, he is sometimes called "Rabbi" meaning a teacher. As a rabbi he should have been married with children but there is no evidence for this in the New Testament, and it is reasonable to assume that he was gay.

Being gay in that Jewish environment he would have felt alone; and as Joseph, his legal father, had probably died when he was very young there was no father-figure in his life. It is therefore understandable that he should form a close personal relationship with God, whom he called "Abba" (an intimate term for "Father") in Mark 14:36. This relationship for Jesus was a loving one.

So, we have a young man who is gay, looks different and feels different, yet is steeped in the Jewish culture of his time and place. Because of his loving nature he finds consolation in his relationship with God. Although not accepted by others he feels accepted by his Creator. It might have been when he was a teenager that he identified with the Suffering Servant of Isaiah 53 who was 'despised and rejected.' Isaiah does not say why the servant was despised, but as someone so different in this very religious environment Jesus probably felt the same. In the gospels there are allusions to the book of Isaiah, and several times Jesus says that the son of man, meaning himself, must suffer. In Mark 10:45 he says that he came to serve and give his life.

When he was about 30, he went to receive John's baptism of repentance. At his baptism Jesus experienced his old life being washed away, although he must still have been aware of his gayness and accepting of it. At the same time something amazing happened: the Holy Spirit entered into him (Mark 1:10). In the Greek text published by the United Bible Society the preposition is εἰς which means 'into'. Jesus felt that the power of his Father was in him.

This man, so different and alone, now had a purpose in life. He could see the meaning of it all: his Father had put him in this time and place to bring in the Kingdom of God. So as a commanding and charismatic figure he embarked on his mission. He told everyone the good news, that the Kingdom of God was near (Mark 1:15), and he was determined to bring it in.

In the Kingdom everyone is loved by the Father and with his love there is acceptance, forgiveness, and healing, just as Jesus had experienced it. When others believed him, remarkable things happened, and large crowds gathered to hear him and bring their sick loved ones to him. The gospel writers all agree that he taught about the Kingdom of God, usually in simple parables so that the people could understand. Some readers, however, have seen Jesus as a passive character in the story, the helpless victim of a cruel world or an innocent man crushed by the wheel of fate. This perception could have derived from Isaiah 53:7 where the Suffering Servant is led like a lamb to the slaughter, but this only applied to Jesus after his arrest in the Garden of Gethsemane. The situation was actually very different because Jesus was in control all the way.

He knew he was the Messiah but not in a political sense. The idea of a coming Messiah was in the Old Testament, and the gospels are full of allusions to passages in it and quotations from it. Some readers have suspected that the gospel writers just made up these connections to support their belief that Jesus was the Messiah. Although this was sometimes the case, as when Matthew referred to Isaiah 7:14 to support Jesus's virginal conception, the allusions are mainly there because Jesus used them in his mission. His stage-managed entry into Jerusalem refers to the prophecy in Zechariah 9:9. His disruption of the business in the Temple, which must have caused the authorities great concern, referred to Jeremiah 7:11. Jesus knew his Hebrew scriptures and he intended to follow them in what he said and did. Even when he was silent before the high priest (Mark 14:61) it was not just a coincidence. He was following the script in Isaiah 53:7. He knew exactly what he was doing.

Jesus arranged everything according to his plan, which was also God's plan. He had provoked the Jewish authorities to kill him, and to make sure he told Judas to inform them where he would be after their fellowship meal, which was the Passover meal in Mark's gospel. The Passover festival was significant for Jesus's purpose because it symbolized the salvation of the people. What is supremely significant is that during this meal Jesus said that the bread he gave them was his body and the wine was his blood, meaning that he would live in them. Like the Suffering Servant he 'poured out his life' (Isaiah 53:12) just as the wine was 'poured out for many' (Mark 14:24). He did this out

3

of love. In the gospels the Greek word for love is ἀγαπη (agape) which means a self-giving concern for others. In this way Jesus gave himself for others and brought in the Kingdom of God.

Jesus would have arranged with Joseph of Arimathea, who was waiting for the Kingdom of God (Mark 15:43), to put his body in his tomb. Jesus expected that when the disciples came together to eat food after his crucifixion, they would realize that he lived in them. He probably did not expect that the Jewish authorities would remove his body to prevent the tomb becoming a rallying site for his followers, but the empty tomb proved to be an added bonus for his purpose, which was to bring in the Kingdom. Actually, it was the Father who arranged for the tomb to be empty. He had prompted the authorities to think of removing the body.

Jesus had to die as the Suffering Servant died. 'He poured out his life unto death.' (Isaiah 53:12) It was God's way of putting his spirit into the hearts of human beings. The Kingdom of God is thus the community of spirit-filled disciples. They are held in God's love, which goes out to the world through them. It is amazing to think that it originated in the love that a gay man felt for his God and God had for him.

Source: https://progressivechristianity.org/resource/jesus-was-different/

****

Reflection:

In this conversation, let's explore Peter's intriguing portrayal of Jesus in his article "JESUS WAS DIFFERENT." Imagine we're sitting in a cozy coffee shop, sipping our favourite brew, and chatting about theology with a touch of curiosity and a sprinkle of humour. While respecting the diverse viewpoints within Christianity, we'll adopt a somewhat traditional stance but keep an open mind to some fresh and thought-provoking perspectives.

Peter's article dives into the idea of Jesus being quite different from what we might traditionally imagine. He suggests that Jesus's early life, before his baptism, set the stage for what Christianity would become. This is a fascinating thought because it prompts us to consider how our own life experiences shape who we are. While traditional Christian teachings emphasize Jesus's divine mission from birth, Peter's perspective invites us to explore new angles. Think of it like looking at a beautiful diamond from different facets – each one shines a bit differently.

Now, Peter suggests that Jesus's birth was natural and that he might have been the illegitimate son of a Roman soldier. This is a bold claim and certainly not the usual Sunday school story. Traditional Christianity holds tightly to the Virgin Birth – a miracle that underscores Jesus's divine nature. While Peter's view humanizes Jesus in a way that makes his struggles relatable, it steps away from the miraculous foundation of Christian faith. It's like adding a plot twist to a well-loved story; it can be exciting but also a bit jarring.

Moreover, the Protoevangelium (Infancy Gospel) of James, an early Christian text, specifically in chapters 1, verses 2-4, doesn't support this position. This text, although not part of the canonical Bible, strongly emphasizes the virgin birth, describing Mary's own miraculous conception and her purity. The Infancy Gospel of James reinforces the traditional narrative of Jesus's divine conception, standing in stark contrast to the idea of a natural, possibly illegitimate birth.

However, considering Peter's perspective, there is an argument to be made for exploring the more human side of Jesus. By presenting Jesus as potentially having a more complex and relatable background, Peter invites readers to connect with Jesus on a deeper, more personal level. This approach can enrich our understanding of Jesus's empathy and compassion, as it suggests that his life experiences were as varied and challenging as those faced by many people today. While this view may diverge from traditional teachings, it encourages a fresh and thought-provoking dialogue about the nature of Jesus's humanity and divinity.

Moving on, Peter talks about Jesus being different in his looks and intelligence, possibly because he had a Roman soldier for a dad. He imagines Jesus as someone who stood out in his community, a bit like that one kid in school who always knew the answers and looked a little different. While it's plausible that Jesus was well-versed in Hebrew scriptures (picture young Jesus having deep theological debates at the temple and flipping tables), tying this to specific cultural interactions, like working in Sepphoris, is speculative. It's like trying to piece together someone's entire life story from a few diary entries – fascinating but incomplete.

Peter also suggests that Jesus's choice to remain single was about his personal inclinations rather than his spiritual purpose; now this is where we tread into sensitive territory. The Gospels don't talk about Jesus's sexuality or intimate relationships as we know them, so any speculation can be a bit like trying to solve a puzzle without all the pieces. Traditional teachings often interpret Jesus's celibacy as a sign of his complete dedication to his divine mission and his singular focus on the Kingdom of God. This perspective emphasizes that Jesus's choice to remain single was about his spiritual purpose rather than his personal inclinations.

However, Peter's suggestion opens an intriguing discussion. In modern times, many people seek to find reflections of their own experiences and identities within the stories of faith. There is a human desire to see oneself in the divine, to feel connected to sacred narratives in a deeply personal way. While there's no direct evidence in the Gospels about Jesus's sexuality, some interpretations of his close relationships, such as the beloved disciple mentioned in the Gospel of John, have sparked debates and curiosity. The term "the disciple whom Jesus loved" has been the subject of much theological and scholarly discussion.

In Greek, the word for "loved" used here can imply a deep, intimate bond, which some modern readers might see as suggesting a special relationship. However, traditionally, this has been understood as a profound spiritual and platonic love. For those in the LGBTQ+ community, seeing Jesus as queer can offer a powerful sense of inclusion and representation within the Christian story. It can be validating to think that Jesus might have understood and shared in their experiences of love and identity.

On the other hand, this perspective challenges longstanding traditional views that have framed Jesus's celibacy within the context of his divine mission and asexuality. This interpretation is less about sexual orientation and more about Jesus's role as a teacher and Savior who transcended earthly desires to focus entirely on his spiritual purpose.

Ultimately, although such suggestions might be seen as radical or unconventional, they invite us to reconsider and broaden our understanding of Jesus's humanity. It encourages a dialogue that respects both the historical and theological contexts of Jesus's life while also acknowledging the diverse ways people today seek to connect with his story. It's a delicate balance, but one that can lead to a richer, more inclusive faith that resonates with the complexities of the human experience.

Peter's idea that Jesus felt alone and formed a close bond with God, whom he called "Abba," is quite touching. This term, "Abba," is an intimate one, akin to saying "Dad." It shows a deep, personal relationship. Peter sees Jesus identifying with the Suffering Servant in Isaiah due to feeling different. This connection is well-established in Christian theology but suggesting it's because Jesus felt marginalized steps into speculative territory. The traditional view sees Jesus's suffering as redemptive for all humanity, not just a personal struggle.

The idea that Jesus's baptism washed away his "old life" and that he was aware of his gayness adds another layer to Peter's narrative. Traditionally, Jesus's baptism is seen as the start of his public ministry and his solidarity with humanity's sin. The Holy Spirit entering him signifies divine empowerment for his mission. It's like the moment a superhero gets their powers – it's about what they'll do with them, not just where they came from.

Peter's view of Jesus as a commanding and charismatic figure with a clear purpose aligns with traditional beliefs. Jesus proclaimed the Kingdom of God – a realm of love, acceptance, and healing. This mission resonates deeply with his own experience of divine love. However, framing it solely within the context of personal feelings of difference can narrow the broader theological significance of his actions. Peter also suggests Jesus was in control of events leading to his death, fulfilling prophecy with strategic actions. This aligns with Gospel accounts but emphasizing Jesus's human planning risks overshadowing the divine orchestration central to Christian belief.

Peter suggests that Jesus's choice to be buried in Joseph of Arimathea's tomb wasn't just a random act. Instead, Jesus might have deliberately arranged this as part of a strategic plan. Think of it as Jesus setting the stage for a bigger message. Peter also proposes that the empty tomb wasn't just a miraculous event but a result of divine intervention. He argues that God nudged the authorities to remove Jesus's body to prevent it from becoming a rallying point for his followers.

From a progressive theological perspective, this interpretation flips the traditional script. Rather than viewing the resurrection as solely a miraculous confirmation of Jesus's divinity, Peter's take paints a picture of Jesus's burial and the empty tomb as purposeful and strategic. It's like Jesus was orchestrating a grand play where every scene had a reason.

This fresh view emphasizes Jesus's active role and divine planning, showing him not just as a passive figure but as someone deeply involved in shaping his mission. It contrasts with traditional beliefs that highlight the resurrection as a direct miracle affirming Jesus's divine nature. Instead, Peter's interpretation invites us to consider how divine action and human strategy interact in the story of Jesus. By rethinking these events, Peter opens up new conversations about Jesus's mission. It's a reminder that understanding these stories can be both a journey through tradition and a fresh exploration of how divine purpose and human action intersect.

It is important to critique Lewis's idea that Jesus may have been same sex attracted. Although the concepts of "gay" and "homosexual" are relatively modern, same-sex attraction has always existed as a part of the spectrum of human sexuality. The term "gay" itself does not necessarily denote same-sex physical intimacy. Some interpretations suggest that Jesus may have experienced same-sex attraction. For instance, the Gospel of John depicts moments such as the beloved disciple leaning on Jesus and Jesus entrusting this disciple with the care of his mother, which some scholars interpret as indicative of a close, possibly romantic, relationship.

It's worth noting that the terms "homosexual" and "gay" were coined only in the late 19th and 20th centuries, respectively. Imposing contemporary labels on historical figures from 2000 years ago is inherently challenging. This complexity must be considered when exploring historical relationships and identities.

In John's Gospel, the portrayal of Jesus can be seen as a reflection of divine love that resonates with queer experiences. Jesus' coming out in this context can be viewed as a powerful symbol for many in the queer community. The Gospel of John is notable for its queer elements, including the fluidity of Jesus' gender expression and his embodiment of divine wisdom. Jesus is depicted as embracing both traditionally feminine and masculine traits, demonstrating a fluidity and submission that aligns with various queer identities.

The narrative of Jesus washing the disciples' feet, for example, highlights his role of humility and submission, which can be seen as a parallel to the roles often ascribed to women or marginalised individuals in patriarchal societies. Jesus' crucifixion, marked by the penetrating force of Roman authority, further symbolises a profound vulnerability and resistance to oppressive systems.

Latina bisexual theologian Marcella Althaus-Reid develops a queer Christology in her interpretation of John 1:14, "The Word became flesh and pitched a tent among us," suggesting a radical inclusivity in Jesus' incarnation. Her work allows for a reimagining of biblical stories through a queer lens. For instance, reading Nicodemus as a closeted gay man and the Samaritan woman as a lesbian who has experienced serial relationships offers a new perspective on these figures.

Similarly, the resurrection of Lazarus has been interpreted by some as a coming-out story, with Lazarus and Jesus' relationship viewed through a lens of queer love. Ben Perkins in 2000[2], employs a hermeneutics of reimagination to present this narrative as a story of self-affirmation and liberation for marginalised individuals.

The beloved disciple, often considered to have a unique and profound connection with Jesus, is frequently interpreted as a representation of homoerotic desire. For nearly two millennia, scholars have explored this relationship as a rare instance of same-sex affection within the Gospels (Goss, 2022; Jennings, 2003; Boisvert,

---

[2] *West, M., Goss, R. E., Bohache, T., & Guest, D. (2006). Queer Bible commentary (p. 554). SCM Press.*

2004)[3]. Gay writer and scholar Donald Boisvert reflects on this dynamic, noting its significance: "It is, however, a beautiful image, a deep and touching affirmation of our central place as gay men in the heart of God" (Boisvert, 2004) [4]. Despite exclusion from some religious institutions, this interpretation suggests a profound place for LGBT+ folk within the heart of God.

In light of these interpretations, can we make a compelling case for a queer Christ? John's Gospel and various scholarly readings offer a vision of Jesus that resonates with queer experiences and identities. By embracing the fluidity of gender, the humility of submission, and the deep, affectionate bonds depicted between Jesus and his followers, we find a Christ who defies conventional boundaries and embodies a radical inclusivity. This queer Christ challenges traditional norms and offers a profound affirmation of diverse identities within the divine narrative. By reconceptualising Jesus through a queer lens, we uncover new dimensions of spiritual connection and liberation, affirming that God's love is indeed expansive and embraces all facets of human experience.

In conclusion, Peter's article offers a fresh perspective, inviting us to critically examine traditional interpretations. Embracing critical inquiry alongside faith allows us to illuminate the enduring complexities of Christ's message and its continuing relevance in our world. This ongoing exploration enriches our understanding of Christian thought and the enduring power of Jesus's teachings for individuals and communities across time. By presenting a fresh perspective on Jesus's life and teachings, Peter encourages believers to reconnect with the core principles of their faith in a more profound and relevant manner.

This revitalization calls for a renewed emphasis on inclusivity, compassion, and social engagement within Christian communities. Peter's progressive interpretations challenge traditional views, urging Christians to embrace diversity and advocate for social justice. By fostering empathy and a deeper understanding of Jesus's message, this approach makes Christianity more resonant with contemporary

---

[3] Ibid., 560.

[4] Ibid., 562.

issues, thereby attracting a broader, more diverse audience and effectively revitalizing Christianity for future generations.

In the end, reimagining Jesus's identity is not about diminishing the divine but about expanding our capacity for empathy, understanding, and connection. By viewing Jesus through various lenses, we honour the depth and complexity of his message, making it ever more relevant in our quest to navigate the profound and often challenging landscape of human experience. This journey invites us to find divinity within our own stories and see the sacred in the diverse tapestry of humanity.

THE HALOED SCHOLAR

2 SIREN CALL
BY DR. PETER E. LEWIS PUBLISHED ON: AUG 4, 2024

I live near a busy road, and I often hear the siren on a police car, ambulance or fire truck. It is an alarming sound declaring to the world that something bad has happened: somebody is in trouble or in danger. When I hear it, my imagination is immediately energized. If it's a police car I think of a road accident and the broken bodies that might be there, or of someone being robbed or murdered. If it's an ambulance I imagine someone so ill or injured that it's a race against time to save them; and if it's a fire truck I see a burning house and wonder what it would be like to lose everything, even loved ones in the fire. Using my imagination in this way is depressing, and it is even more so when I realize that there is nothing I can do when I hear the siren. Oh, if only I could be there to help and comfort those so hurt.

But all is not doom and gloom because I also think of the men and women in the police car, ambulance or fire truck. What wonderful people they are, rushing to save their fellow human beings! I might be able to imagine the scene that will confront them when they arrive at their destination, but for them it will be stark reality: a bleeding mangled body in a crushed vehicle, an infant burnt in the fire, a young woman with multiple stab wounds. I will not go on. Enough has been said to explain why so many of these first responders develop PTSD (post-traumatic stress disorder). It is a serious disabling condition that can be life-long. The community is asking a lot from these good people to do what they do.

Recently I had a paradigm shift in my thinking. I changed my whole response to the sound of the siren because I realized that there was certainly something I could do: I could pray. Now, when I hear the siren I say a simple prayer, usually three words, "Help them, Lord." Sometimes I am more specific, and I might say, "Be with the paramedics, Lord." It only takes a few seconds, but instead of being depressed I feel part of the whole positive response to the event.

I am a progressive Christian. I don't believe in the virgin birth or the bodily resurrection, but I do believe that there is a certain validity in prayer. I am not saying that you can cure sick people or perform miracles by praying. You can't. When I pray, I am talking to myself, but as a Christian I have in the depth of my being something divine, the Holy Spirit. Therefore, when I pray, I am conversing with God. I speak to Him or Her and I am open to receive intimations of a spiritual nature. But how can this prayer have any effect beyond the individual?

Let me digress for a moment. I had a cousin who never married but she had a cat which she called Jazz because she had been a teacher of dancing. She loved the cat like a child. When she was 95, she became completely blind and had to leave her home which was next to a park and go into a nursing home. The cat was able to survive in the park because a neighbour put food out for it at night. But someone noticed the old cat in the park and contacted the city council to take it away. The neighbour who fed the cat heard that the council men were trying to catch it and she hid it in her home till the crisis was over. When I phoned my cousin to tell her that Jazz was safe, she was very distressed because she just knew that the cat was in danger. There is no way that she could have known this, and I realized that there are aspects of our lives that we do not and cannot understand. I have since heard stories of mothers who just knew that their children were in serious trouble, and knowing about my cousin and her cat, I believe them.

I know it is trivial and it could all have been just co-incidence, but it strengthened my belief that the Holy Spirit has both an individual and a group function in the world. As many Christians say in church every Sunday, "We are the body of Christ in the world. His spirit is with us." In some mysterious way the Holy Spirit connects all Christians.

Therefore, I call on every Christian, wherever they are in the world, to say a simple prayer when they hear the siren. It might help people in some way that we do not understand. It might influence the thinking of the first responders in a positive way. In any case it would increase the intensity of compassion in the people praying and that would be of benefit to the world. Apathy and inertia result from lack of imagination. Compassion depends on it, and exercising the human imagination increases Love in the world.

Instead of being annoyed or depressed by the alarming sound, we can all make a positive response to the distressing situation that the siren is heralding. At night when we watch the TV news and see road accidents and criminals in handcuffs, it is too late to do anything. When you hear the siren call, that is the time to pray.

Source: https://progressivechristianity.org/resource/siren-cal/

****

Reflection:

Peter's reflection in "Siren Call" offers more than just a theological exploration; it provides a practical approach to integrating spirituality into our daily lives. He encourages us to view the sound of a siren— not as a mere disruption, but as a chance for spiritual action.

Instead of letting the piercing sound of an emergency siren overwhelm us with anxiety, Peter proposes using it as a prompt for prayer. This simple yet profound practice allows us to transform our initial concern into a meaningful connection with the needs of others. Whether it's a quick prayer like "Help them, Lord" or a more specific plea like "Be with the paramedics," Peter suggests that these moments can become opportunities for compassion.

His approach is refreshingly accessible. By turning the everyday occurrence of hearing a siren into a cue for prayer, Peter makes spirituality a living, breathing part of our routine. This practice isn't just an academic exercise; it's a personal and transformative act that enriches our daily lives with deeper connection and empathy.

Peter's call resonates with the comforting promise of Isaiah 41:10: "So do not fear, for I am with you; do not be dismayed, for I am your God. I will strengthen you and help you; I will uphold you with my righteous right hand." This verse reassures us of divine support and encourages us to extend that support to others. By responding to sirens with prayer, we align our personal spirituality with a broader divine framework of care.

His reflection invites us to weave spirituality into everyday moments, making our practices not only more responsive but also more meaningful. Peter's idea demonstrates how progressive Christian values can be applied practically. It's about transforming moments of distress into opportunities for compassionate action, connecting our individual prayers with a larger network of empathy and support.

In essence, Peter turns a potentially unsettling experience into a spiritual opportunity. Instead of succumbing to feelings of helplessness when a siren blares, we can engage with our faith and each other in a simple yet profound way. This practice reminds us that spirituality doesn't always need to be grand or complicated; often, it's about seizing small, everyday moments to offer care and connection.

So, next time you hear a siren, remember Isaiah 41:10 and take a moment for a quick prayer. It's a small act, but it can significantly enhance how we connect with and support those around us, turning a moment of alarm into an opportunity for spiritual engagement and compassionate action.

JOURNEY OF REVELATION

3 THE ENDING OF LUKE'S GOSPEL
By Dr. Peter E. Lewis Published On: April 2, 2021

I have been thinking about the ending of Luke's gospel. Luke's ending (24:1-53) is based on Mark's ending (16:1-20) and is a modified and magnified version of it. When this is realized one can work out how Luke's ending developed into its final form. Also, one needs to understand that during this period of development a pro-Peter group had become powerful in Rome.

Consider Mark 16:12,13. Two disciples were walking in the country when Jesus appeared to them in a different form. They returned to Jerusalem and reported it to the rest, but they did not believe them. In Luke 24:33-35 we read: *They got up and returned at once to Jerusalem. There they found the Eleven and those with them, assembled together and saying "It is true! The Lord has risen and has appeared to Simon." Then the two told what had happened on the way, and how Jesus was recognized by them when he broke the bread.* (NIV) Notice how incongruous are the words, *and has appeared to Simon.* Nowhere in the gospels is this appearance to Peter mentioned. The words have obviously been inserted here so that the first appearance of the risen Christ was to Peter, not to Mary Magdalene as in Mark 16:9 or to the two returned disciples.

Next consider the word "saying" in Luke 24:34. In the Greek text it is in the accusative case and therefore refers to the Eleven, but think of the enormous difference it makes to the meaning of the passage if it is in the nominative case. Then it refers to the two disciples who had recognized Jesus when he broke the bread. In Codex Bezae, a 5th century uncial manuscript, "saying" is in the nominative case.

Next consider the word "assembled" in Luke 24:33. The Greek word occurs only here in the New Testament, but it does occur in the Septuagint and in Classical Greek where it has the connotation of mustering troops. The word seems out of place here, and raises the question why the disciples were together in Jerusalem at this time. In Mark's gospel the situation is plainly stated: the Eleven had come together to eat food (Mark 16:14). It was their first post-crucifixion meal. If Luke 24:33-35 is read with Mark's account in mind, the text becomes: *They got up and returned at once to Jerusalem. There they found the Eleven and those with them as they were eating. The two disciples said, "The Lord has risen indeed!" Then they told what had happened on the way, and how Jesus was recognized by them when he broke the bread.* Then Jesus appeared and the Eleven were startled and frightened.

Realizing that Luke's version was based on Mark's account makes a tremendous difference. It means that although at first the Eleven did not believe the two disciples, they had the same experience when the bread was broken. It enables modern Christians to realize that they are those disciples on the way to Emmaus. When the bread was broken, *then their eyes were opened and they recognized him, and he disappeared from their sight.* (Luke 24:31)

** The group who inserted the appearance to Peter wanted to squash the meal idea because they believed in the bodily resurrection of Jesus. The story of the two disciples on the way to Emmaus described a spiritual resurrection. For them Jesus appeared when they ate the bread because he had said that it was his body. Jesus meant that he would live in his disciples. The pro-Peter group confirmed their belief in the bodily resurrection in Luke 24:39 when Jesus said to touch him, and in 24:42 when he eats fish.

In 1 Cor. 15:5 Paul said that Christ appeared first to Peter.

Women, of course, were excluded because their testimony was worthless. Probably it was at the Council of Jerusalem in 49 AD when Peter, James (Jesus' brother) and others claimed that they had seen the risen Christ.

Source: https://progressivechristianity.org/resource/the-ending-of-lukes-gospel/

****

Reflection:

I've been mulling over Peter's thoughts on how Luke wraps up his Gospel. Peter suggests that Luke's ending (24:1-53) is an expanded version of Mark's ending (16:1-20). By understanding this, we can trace how Luke's conclusion came to be, especially considering the influence of a pro-Peter group in Rome during that time.

Think about Mark 16:12-13, where two disciples are walking in the country when Jesus appears to them in a different form. They go back to Jerusalem to report this, but no one believes them. Now, look at Luke 24:33-35. The disciples return to Jerusalem and find the Eleven and others saying, "It is true! The Lord has risen and has appeared to Simon." Here, Lewis notes that this mention of Jesus appearing to Simon seems out of place because no other Gospel mentions this. It appears that these words could have been inserted to make Peter the first witness to the risen Christ, overshadowing Mary Magdalene's encounter in Mark 16:9.

Peter dives deeper into the Greek text. In Luke 24:34, the word "saying" in the accusative case refers to the Eleven. But if it were in the nominative case, it would refer to the two disciples. This small change makes a big difference in the passage's meaning. Interestingly, Codex Bezae, a 5th-century manuscript, has "saying" in the nominative case, which supports the two disciples.

The Greek word for "assembled" in Luke 24:33 is unique in the New Testament but common in the Septuagint and Classical Greek, where it implies mustering troops. This odd choice raises questions about why the disciples were together in Jerusalem. Mark's Gospel is straightforward: the Eleven gathered to eat (Mark 16:14), their first meal after the crucifixion. Reading Luke with Mark in mind, the text becomes: "They got up and returned to Jerusalem. There they found

18

the Eleven and others eating. The two disciples said, 'The Lord has risen indeed!' Then they told what happened, and how Jesus was recognized by them when he broke the bread. Then Jesus appeared, and the Eleven were startled and frightened."

Realizing that Luke's account builds on Mark's makes a big difference. Although the Eleven initially didn't believe the two disciples, they had the same experience when the bread was broken. It helps modern Christians see themselves as those disciples on the road to Emmaus. When the bread was broken, their eyes were opened, and they recognized Jesus.

Peter's argument is that a pro-Peter group edited the text to downplay the meal idea and emphasize the bodily resurrection. They wanted to counter the spiritual resurrection depicted in the Emmaus story, where Jesus is recognized in the breaking of bread, symbolizing his continued presence in his followers. This group reinforced their belief in the bodily resurrection by including Jesus asking to be touched (Luke 24:39) and eating fish (Luke 24:42).

Paul's statement in 1 Corinthians 15:5 that Christ appeared first to Peter (excluding women's testimony because it was considered unreliable) probably stems from the Council of Jerusalem in 49 AD, where Peter, James, and others claimed to have seen the risen Christ.
Lewis's take on Luke's Gospel, proposing that it's an expanded version of Mark's influenced by a pro-Peter faction, opens up a lot to think about. Luke's Gospel is rich with themes of salvation, the role of women, social justice, and inclusion, and these themes are particularly vivid in its conclusion.

Despite differing scholarly opinions on its origins, Luke's Gospel was widely circulated among early Christian communities, each interpreting Jesus' resurrection through their theological lenses. This diversity highlights the varied beliefs within early Christianity and Luke's contribution to these theological debates.

Understanding the complex historical context of early Christianity, shaped by Roman imperialism, Jewish traditions, and cultural influences, helps us see why Luke might have portrayed Peter's encounter with Jesus in the way he did. Roman societal structures likely influenced early Christian leadership models and theological emphases, shedding light on why Peter's role and the bodily resurrection were so significant.

Peter Lewis's hypothesis about the influence of a pro-Peter faction invites us to reconsider how early Christian texts were shaped. It encourages us to look at the bigger picture of theological motivations and historical accuracy, acknowledging the diversity of early Christian views on resurrection and the evolving theological debates within the early Church.

In summary, Peter's insights challenge us to delve deeper into the textual, theological, and historical dimensions of Luke's Gospel. By exploring these layers, we gain a richer understanding of how early Christian communities interpreted and transmitted their faith, and how these foundational texts continue to shape our theological discussions today.

PRISMATIC PURGE

4 JESUS AND THE SACRIFICIAL SYSTEM
By Dr. Peter E. Lewis Published On: January 21, 2022

The religious culture in which Jesus lived was the sacrificial culture centred on the temple in Jerusalem. It provided the background to his thinking and that of most other Jews including Paul, and the idea of sacrifice continued to influence the thinking of the first Christians. Paul spells this out in his first letter to the Corinthians: "For what I received I passed on to you as of first importance that Christ died for our sins according to the Scriptures." (1 Cor 15:3)

In the "Scriptures" the prophet Isaiah had written that an individual would be an offering for sin and bear the sin of many. (53:10-12). Jesus took on the role of this individual who became known as the Suffering Servant. In the gospels Jesus says that the son of man (meaning himself) must suffer and be killed. (Mark 8:31). He says he came to serve and give his life as a ransom for many. (Mark 10:44) Accordingly Jesus and the first Christians thought of the Christ event in terms of sacrifice.

In the time of Jesus, animals of various kinds were sacrificed in the temple, which must have been more like an abattoir than a place of worship. Today the whole idea of making sacrifices to appease a wrathful god is abhorrent to modern Christians because it is not in keeping with the loving God that they encounter in Jesus Christ. Even the emphasis on sin seems out of keeping with their experience.

Sin is not all the naughty things that we do from time to time. It is everything that separates us from God. Paul said something similar in his letter to the Romans: "Everything that does not come from faith is sin." (Rom 14:23b) So if sin is removed, we are with God.

Being with God is what Jesus meant by the Kingdom of God. It was not something that happened to good people when they died. By taking on the role of the Suffering Servant Jesus believed that he would bring in the Kingdom of God. According to Isaiah, the Suffering Servant "will justify many". (Isaiah 53:11b) They will be acceptable to God: they will be with God.

It is important to understand that the sacrificial system was just the background to what needed to be revealed. It was a stepping stone that enabled a further important step to be made. It was the stage on which a drama of revelation could be performed.

In the Kingdom of God everyone is loved by God. With this love there is acceptance, forgiveness, and healing. The key idea is 'love' (Greek: agape), which in the New Testament means a self-giving concern for others. Jesus does more that talk about the Kingdom of God, he demonstrates what this kingdom love is by caring for others, and he does this in a self-giving way. Actually, he gives himself completely: as Isaiah says, "He poured out his life unto death." (Isaiah 53:12)

As modern Christians we do not have to sacrifice animals or anything. We can abhor the old system because it is irrelevant today. What is essential is that we have to follow Jesus's example and behave in a way that overcomes selfishness. We must be open to the world, and love as Jesus loved. The key idea in Buddhism is overcoming self, and this is also what Christianity is about. The Buddha was not interested in gods, but Jesus used the prevailing Jewish system to reveal the loving God that he believed in, and which Christians believe was with him and in him.

Source: https://progressivechristianity.org/resource/jesus-and-the-sacrificial-system/

****

Reflection:

You know how Peter has this knack for diving deep into theology and making sense of it all, right? Well, his take on Jesus and the sacrificial system is no different. It's like he's our guide through this ancient world of rituals and sacrifices, showing us how Jesus flipped the script.

First off, Peter sets the stage in Jerusalem, where the temple was more like a busy butcher shop than a peaceful place of worship. Sacrifices were the way people thought they could mend their relationship with God. But Jesus, being the radical he was, had a different idea.

Peter points out how Jesus saw himself as the Suffering Servant mentioned in Isaiah. Imagine this: Jesus knew he had to suffer and die, but he believed it was for a greater purpose. He wasn't just following the old rules; he was redefining them. When Jesus talked about giving his life as a ransom for many, he was showing a new way to connect with God—through love and self-giving, not through rituals and animal sacrifices.

Now, Peter also touches on how modern Christians often find the idea of sacrifices to appease a wrathful God pretty disturbing. I mean, who wants to think of God as someone who needs appeasing, right? It feels out of step with the loving, accepting God we meet in Jesus.

But here's where Peter gets really interesting. He explains that sin isn't just about our little mistakes or naughty behaviour. It's anything that separates us from God. Paul even said that anything not coming from faith is sin. So, if Jesus' sacrifice wipes away that separation, it's like opening the door to the Kingdom of God right here and now, not just after we die.

Peter's take is that the old sacrificial system was just the backdrop for Jesus to reveal something much bigger. It was like the stage for a new drama of revelation. Jesus' message was all about love (agape in Greek), which means a self-giving concern for others. And he didn't just preach it—he lived it, even to the point of death.

In today's world, Peter argues, we don't need to sacrifice animals or anything else. What we need is to follow Jesus' example of overcoming selfishness and loving others. It's like Buddhism's idea of overcoming the self, but with a focus on a loving God who is with us and in us.

Peter's insights are supported by biblical passages like Mark 8:31 and Mark 10:45, where Jesus talks about his suffering and death. It's clear that Jesus saw his sacrifice as a transformative act of love, not just a ritualistic obligation.

Of course, there are always different perspectives in theology. Some might say Peter overlooks aspects like divine justice or other interpretations of atonement. But that's the beauty of theological discussion, right? It's like a big, ongoing conversation where we can learn from each other.

In the end, Peter's focus on sacrificial love is a powerful reminder of what it means to follow Jesus. It's not about clinging to old rituals but about living a life of love, forgiveness, and openness. And for progressive Christians like us, who see Jesus as someone who never marginalized anyone, this message is incredibly relevant.

So, next time you're pondering the deeper meanings of sacrifice and love, think of Peter's perspective. It's like he's offering us a new lens to see the timeless story of Jesus in a way that resonates with our modern lives.

EMANATIONS OF WISDOM

5 JESUS AND THE MIDRASHIC SYSTEM

By Dr. Peter E. Lewis Published On: April 2, 2021

In his important book, *Liberating the Gospels: Reading the Bible with Jewish Eyes*, John Shelby Spong pointed out that the followers of Jesus who wrote about his life were all Jews. Even Luke, according to Spong, was a convert who was steeped in Jewish thoughts. In trying to understand the Christ Event they searched the Hebrew scriptures for "the symbols and the stories of their sacred past." (page 309) They were searching for some frame of reference, and they found it particularly in the figure of the Suffering Servant as described in Isaiah 52:13 – 53:12. "This figure was clearly used again and again in the developing Christian story." (page 224) Explaining events with reference to people from the sacred past was the midrashic method that the gospel writers used. The Jewish midrashic technique was "opening the scriptures so that Jesus could be seen as the fulfillment of the law and the prophets." (page 215)

Spong emphasized that everyone writing about Jesus was steeped in this Midrashic way of making sense of it all. Actually, every Jew who thought about Jesus would have been caught up in this method of interpretation. What Spong did not realize was that Jesus himself must have thought in this way. It is inconceivable that Jesus was not also steeped in the Midrashic way of thinking, and once this is realized a whole new understanding is opened up.

Jesus was not a passive character in the story. He was in control all the way, and he saw his path forward in terms of "the symbols and the stories of their sacred past." In the article that I wrote last year for Progressive Christianity entitled 'Jesus was different' I argued that Jesus identified with the Suffering Servant even before he began his mission at age 30. Jesus believed that by taking on the role of the Suffering Servant he would bring in the Kingdom of God. He would be an offering for sin and bear the sin of many. Through him the will of the Lord would prosper.

Jesus being the Suffering Servant was not a late development in the gospel story. In referring to the symbol of the Suffering Servant, Spong wrote, "This individualized portrait of a nation that was victimized, but nonetheless affirmed by God, was quickly incorporated by the early Christians into the story of Jesus." (page 251) In his First Letter to the Corinthians written only about 24 years after the crucifixion Paul wrote, "For what I received I passed on to you as of first importance: that Christ died for our sins according to the Scriptures." (1 Cor 15:3) In his mission Jesus stressed that the son of man, meaning himself, must suffer, and in Mark 10:45 he said that he came to serve and give his life.

If Jesus willingly took on the role of the Suffering Servant, what motivated him to do it? I believe it was love. He did it out of love for each and every one of us. It was a self-giving sacrificial love. As Paul wrote in his letter to the Galatians, "I live by faith in the Son of God, who loved me and gave himself for me." (Gal 2:20) Spong believed that "Jesus lived the love of God. . . That love of God which Christians believe they meet in Jesus has one purpose: It is to invite us to be and to love us into being loving people." (page 332) This was what Jesus meant by the Kingdom of God.

Source: https://progressivechristianity.org/resource/jesus-and-the-midrashic-method/

****

Reflection:

Peter's article, "Jesus and the Midrashic System," got me thinking about how Jesus' teachings line up with the Jewish Midrashic tradition. If you're like me, someone who finds joy in the depth of theology but prefers it without the heavy jargon, then this conversation is for you.

Peter talks about how Jesus used storytelling techniques, like parables, to share deep spiritual truths. These parables are quite similar to the Midrashic methods that ancient Jewish scholars used to explain and explore the Hebrew Scriptures. Basically, they used stories and allegories to dig deeper into the meaning of the texts. Think of it like using fairy tales to teach kids life lessons – but on a much more profound level.

One of the important things Peter highlights is how early Christians, who were Jewish, used these Midrashic techniques to connect Jesus' life with the Hebrew Scriptures. This wasn't just a way to make sense of things; it was also a bridge for Jewish and Christian audiences to understand Jesus in the context of their shared history and beliefs.

Now, our friend John Shelby Spong, who isn't afraid to challenge traditional views, would probably nod along with Peter's exploration. But Spong might remind us not to box Jesus in with just one interpretive method. Jesus' teachings were radical and transformative, shaking up social norms and religious practices of his time. Spong often focuses on how Jesus promoted inclusivity, social justice, and a radical love that transcends the limits of traditional Jewish expectations.

Spong might also urge us to look at the bigger picture of Jesus' ministry. It wasn't just about theological insights but also addressing real-world issues like economic inequality, political oppression, and the marginalization of various groups. By looking at these broader implications, we can appreciate the full scope of Jesus' mission and its relevance to today's world.

The Midrashic tradition itself is fascinating. It's all about finding deeper meanings in scriptures through storytelling and ethical insights. Early Christian writers used these methods to interpret Jesus' life and mission in light of the Old Testament prophecies. For instance, Matthew's Gospel is full of Old Testament references that show Jesus as the fulfillment of Jewish messianic expectations.

Comparing these Midrashic interpretations with other methods used by Jewish and early Christian scholars highlights the richness and diversity of theological thought. It shows us how various traditions have shaped our understanding of who Jesus is and what he stood for.

Despite its richness, the Midrashic approach does have its critics. Some might question whether it's the best way to understand Jesus' teachings. This is why rigorous scholarship and sensitivity to historical context are essential when interpreting ancient texts.

But here's the thing: Midrashic interpretations of Jesus can deepen our faith by revealing the Jewish roots of his teachings. They remind us of the imperatives of compassion, forgiveness, and the transformative power of sacrificial love that are at the heart of Jesus' message.

Adding another layer to this conversation, if we look at Peter's article through N.T. Wright's lens, we get even more depth. Wright might emphasize Jesus' claims about the Kingdom of God and his identity as the Messiah. While Peter focuses on how Jesus' sacrificial death fits into the Midrashic tradition, Wright might highlight the broader implications of Jesus' atoning work and its impact on the New Testament narrative.

Central to Peter's argument is the idea that Jesus saw himself as the Suffering Servant mentioned in Isaiah. This role was not just something that happened to Jesus but something he actively embraced as part of his mission to fulfill God's will and reconcile humanity. This interpretation is backed by early Christian writings, like Paul's assertion in 1 Corinthians 15:3 that Christ died for our sins according to the Scriptures.

In essence, Peter's article invites us to look at Jesus through the Midrashic lens, enriching our understanding of his teachings and identity. It's a call to appreciate the theological complexities and the profound love that Jesus embodied.

Peter's work encourages ongoing exploration of Midrashic studies and their relevance to contemporary theology. It's an exciting invitation to delve deeper into how these interpretations can inform our understanding of ethics, eschatology (belief concerning death), and interfaith dialogue today.

As you reflect on Peter's exploration of Jesus through the Midrashic tradition, consider how this approach might enhance our grasp of Jesus' teachings and their significance in our discussions today.

CELESTIAL CARESS

6 WHO OR WHAT IS GOD?
By Dr. Peter E. Lewis Published On: July 9, 2022

I do not know. Nobody knows. There is no certainty in religion: faith and doubt must go hand-in-hand. Faith derives mainly from the innate human search for meaning, and although our life experiences are so different, inevitably we ask, "What's it all about, Alfie?" Fortunately, in human life, there is the puzzling little additive called intuition, which occasionally pricks us to think that there may be more than just the material world. It alerts us to the Mystery in which we exist.

Concerning the nature of God, anthropomorphism does not worry me because in the Mystery there is humanness. We are in the Mystery. We can do no more than try to apprehend it in human terms, but as Martin Buber argued, any type of I-It relationship with God should be avoided. In the Mystery the dialogue is I-You.

Abstract ideas about God such as panentheism sound reasonable, even scientific like physics, but they do not mean much. Although I like the idea of everything in God and God in everything, it is very metaphysical. Religion is largely a human construct, and I think it is better to approach the Mystery from the human side.

As the psalmist wondered, what are we as human beings? We are not angelic beings. Our lives are limited in time and space, and our understanding is limited. As Christians we believe that the key to understanding our situation is Jesus. He emerged out of the environment of 1st-century Judaism, and using the tools at hand he constructed a religious edifice based on the assumption that at the heart of the Mystery there is something positive. Call it Love, goodness, holiness or whatever. As Christians we joyfully enter the wonderful edifice that Jesus created.

The main 'tool' that Jesus used in constructing Christianity was given to him by the prophet Isaiah, and that was the idea of the Suffering Servant. Jesus took on this role believing that the Kingdom of God would result. What is truly mind-blowing is that it did. The establishment of the Kingdom of God confirmed Jesus's belief and Isaiah's prophecy.

Although we do not know the exact nature of God or whatever is at the heart of the Mystery, we can be confident that it is something good. As Christians we have taken the leap of faith and are in the Kingdom of God. We are "alive to God in Christ Jesus" and with the words of Frances Havergal's hymn we sing, "Take my heart, it is thine own; it shall be thy royal throne."

Source: https://progressivechristianity.org/resource/who-or-what-is-god-2/

****

Reflection:

I was reflecting on Peter's article, "Who or What is God?", and it struck me as a really heartfelt exploration of one of humanity's most profound questions. Peter starts with a humble admission: "I do not know. Nobody knows." This sets the tone for a journey into the mysterious, where faith and doubt walk hand-in-hand.

Peter's honesty here is refreshing. It's like when you're with friends, and someone admits they don't have all the answers — it creates an open, trusting space. Faith, as Peter puts it, comes from our deep-seated need to find meaning. Even though our experiences differ, we all end up asking, "What's it all about?" This question is universal, isn't it?

Peter touches on something quite profound with intuition. Sometimes, we just feel there's more to life than what we see. This intuition nudges us towards the Mystery, the sense that there's something beyond the material world.

When Peter talks about anthropomorphism – that's a fancy way of saying we picture God in human terms – he's okay with it. He suggests that since we are part of this Mystery, it makes sense to understand it in ways that are familiar to us. But he's also careful, like Martin Buber, to say we should avoid seeing God as an object (an "I-It" relationship) and instead engage with God as a "You," a presence we relate to personally.

Peter is a bit sceptical about abstract ideas like panentheism – the notion that God is in everything and everything is in God. He finds it too metaphysical, preferring to start with human experiences. This is where he might part ways with more mystical traditions that find value in such concepts.

In reflecting on the human condition, Peter asks with the psalmist, "What are we as human beings?" We're not angels, and our understanding is limited. Yet, as Christians, we believe that Jesus gives us a key to understanding our situation. Jesus, emerging from first-century Judaism, used the tools of his time to build a faith that centres on something inherently positive at the heart of the Mystery – call it Love, goodness, or holiness.

Peter highlights how Jesus embraced the role of the Suffering Servant from Isaiah, believing that this path would lead to the Kingdom of God. And astonishingly, it did. The Kingdom of God came into being, confirming Jesus' belief and Isaiah's prophecy.

Peter's insistence on the goodness at the heart of the Mystery resonates deeply with Christian belief. Even though we can't fully grasp God's nature, we can be confident that it's something good. This leap of faith places us in the Kingdom of God, alive to God in Christ Jesus.

While Peter's reflections are insightful, they do raise a few points for further discussion. For instance, when he says, "nobody knows" about God, it might seem like he's dismissing centuries of theological inquiry. But perhaps he's simply emphasizing that any understanding of God must remain humble and open to mystery. It's not about having all the answers but about being willing to explore and question.

Peter's acceptance of anthropomorphism is practical, but we shouldn't ignore the challenges it poses. How do we balance our human ways of understanding with the idea that God transcends human comprehension? It's a tricky dance between what's familiar and what's beyond us.

When Peter says religion is largely a human construct, he's acknowledging the cultural and historical influences on our beliefs. But let's not forget the transcendent aspects that many faith traditions hold dear – the moments of divine revelation that go beyond human construction.

Peter's focus on Jesus as the key to understanding God is central to Christian belief, but exploring other perspectives within Christianity, like liberation theology, could enrich this discussion. These perspectives highlight Jesus' role in advocating for justice and challenging social inequalities.

Finally, Peter's conclusion, that despite not knowing the exact nature of God, we can trust in its goodness, is a comforting thought. It aligns with the Christian belief in a benevolent Creator. But engaging with diverse experiences, including those from other faith traditions and marginalized communities, can deepen our understanding of this Mystery.

In sum, Peter's article invites us into a thoughtful conversation about God. It's like sitting down with a friend over a cup of tea, pondering life's big questions. We don't need all the answers to appreciate the journey. And in this journey, we find solace, purpose, and a sense of belonging. So, let's keep exploring, questioning, and embracing the Mystery, knowing that in our seeking, we find something profoundly good.

HERE AND NOW

7 NO SECOND COMING

By Dr. Peter E. Lewis Published On: January 8, 2024

As we approach 2024, once again our minds are drawn to speculation about what lies ahead of us. Dr Peter Lewis reflects on the faulty teaching about the Second Coming that takes away our responsibility for following Jesus' teaching and taking responsibility for all humanity and the place we inhabit. All the best for the year ahead as we enter our 24th year at the UC FORUM.

The Second Coming of Christ is an erroneous idea that developed among Christians in the last third of the first century AD. It weakened the assurance that the first Christians had that the kingdom of God had come.

Jesus took on the role of the Suffering Servant as described in Isaiah 52:13-53:12 and in some of the psalms, and as the Messiah giving his life in accordance with that role, he expected the kingdom of God to come. In Mark 9:1 he says that some standing with him will not die before they see the kingdom of God come in power, and

34

he was not referring to the Transfiguration.

In some of his parables he describes what the kingdom is like, but they are rather vague and only give hints as to what to expect. Probably Jesus himself had no clear idea of what would happen, but he was confident that people and God would be brought together, and he (the Son of Man) would be sitting at the right hand of God, which was what he told the high priest in Mark 14:62.

In Mark 16:19 Jesus is sitting at the right hand of God and the kingdom of God has come for those who believe. During his lifetime the good news was that the kingdom of God was near, but with his 'sacrifice of love' it had come.

The first followers of Jesus realized that they were in the kingdom. As Paul or whoever wrote the letter to the Colossians said, "[God] has rescued us from the dominion of darkness and brought us into the kingdom of the Son he loves" (Col 1:14). In the kingdom God rules with Christ at his right hand, and a way to understand this is to think of human existence as being in both the objective and the subjective. Jesus in the form of the Holy Spirit is prompting our thoughts in the subjective.

The Lord's Supper is the central sacrament in Christianity, and those who believe in Jesus Christ take him into themselves: the Holy Spirit enters their minds, and they are in the kingdom of God. The sacrament is repeated to remind Christians of who Jesus was and what he did. To say that the kingdom has not yet come and to hope for a miraculous event in the sky, as described in 1 Thess 4:13-18, is to deny what Jesus did on the cross.

Some scholars think that 1 Thessalonians was the first letter that Paul wrote, but although some parts might be from his hand, the rest was written much later, probably during or soon after the First Jewish War (66-70 AD). In 2 Cor 3:17b Paul writes that "where the Spirit of the Lord is, there is freedom," but in 1 Thess 5:12 it is written that Christians have people over them in the Lord to admonish them. In 1 Thess 2:16 the author says that the wrath of God has come upon the Jews. Surely this is a reference to their defeat in the Jewish War.

In 1 Cor 15:24-26 Paul talks about the end of time when Christ's reign has been successful, and he hands over the kingdom to God the Father. This is a different situation from the Second Coming as described in 1 Thess 4:13-18, which was perceived as imminent.

To understand how the idea of an imminent Second Coming arose in the early Church one needs to consider the historical circumstances. When Mark wrote his gospel, which concluded with Jesus sitting at the right hand of God, conditions were stable, and Christianity was spreading in the Roman Empire. He was writing before the fire in Rome, which occurred in 64 AD. Nero blamed the Christians and they were horribly persecuted. Then in 66 AD the Jewish War began. It was a terrible time for everyone involved, and it is understandable that some Christians would look to Jesus to come again and save them.

But being in the kingdom of God means responsibility. It means living as Jesus exemplified and commanded us to do, in order to consolidate his reign and change the world. It means living in the present, facing the current circumstances and doing something about them if they are in the dominion of darkness. Burying our heads in the sand, saying that the kingdom has not come and hoping for a Second Coming, is the opposite of what Jesus was about.

In Galatians 2:20 Paul said, "Christ lives in me." Actually, he lives in everyone who believes. With Christ in their hearts Christians are in the kingdom of God, and their task is to increase the kingdom. When times are bad and wars are raging, their response should not be to pray for a Second Coming but to be Christ in the world.

Source: https://progressivechristianity.org/resource/no-second-coming/

****

Reflection:

Peter's article, "No Second Coming," is like a breath of fresh air in the world of Christian eschatology. He challenges the traditional belief in a future Second Coming of Christ, and instead, he suggests that the Kingdom of God is already here. It's a bold stance, and it shakes things up, so let's dive in together and see what we think.

First off, Peter argues that the idea of a Second Coming didn't pop up until later in the first century. He thinks it might have been a way for early Christians to cope with tough times, like the persecution under Nero or the Jewish War. Imagine you're part of a small, oppressed group, and you start looking for a sign of hope. A future return of Jesus might sound pretty comforting, right? But Peter suggests this kind of thinking might have led us away from the original message of Jesus: that the Kingdom of God is already here, among us.

Now, this might seem like a radical idea, but Peter isn't just making stuff up. He digs into the Bible to back up his points. For example, he brings up Mark 9:1, where Jesus says some people standing with him will see the Kingdom of God come in power before they die. Peter interprets this not as a hint of a future event, but as something that was happening right then. Jesus was bringing people closer to God, and through his life, death, and resurrection, the Kingdom of God was already breaking into the world.

Peter also tackles some of Paul's letters, like 1 Thessalonians. He argues that parts of these letters might have been written later, during or after the Jewish War, which could explain the different tones and messages. For instance, Paul talks about freedom in the Spirit in 2 Corinthians, but in 1 Thessalonians, there's this hierarchy and talk of God's wrath. It's like reading two different authors! Peter suggests that this could mean some parts were added later to address the crises of the time.

But what does this all mean for us today? Well, Peter is essentially saying that waiting around for a miraculous Second Coming isn't what Jesus wanted. Instead, he calls us to live out the Kingdom of God right now. This means taking responsibility, loving our neighbours, and working for justice and peace. It's a call to action, not a call to sit and wait.

Peter's perspective is especially relevant in today's world. We're facing huge challenges like climate change, social inequality, political instability, and global health crises. Thinking of the Kingdom of God as something already here urges us to act now, to make a difference in the world. It's a powerful reminder that our faith should be active and engaged, not passive and waiting for some future event.

For those of us who resonate with queer theology, Peter's message is particularly empowering. Jesus didn't marginalize people; he brought them in, loved them, and showed them their worth. Seeing the Kingdom of God as a present reality means we're called to do the same. It's about creating an inclusive, just, and loving world right here and now.

And let's not forget the role of the Holy Spirit. Peter points out that with the Holy Spirit in us, we're already in the Kingdom of God. This isn't some future promise; it's a current reality. It's like having a little bit of heaven in our hearts, guiding us to live out Jesus' teachings in our everyday lives. So, instead of praying for a Second Coming, we should be praying for the strength and wisdom to be Christ in the world today.

Now, let's be honest, Peter's outright dismissal of the Second Coming might be a bit too much for some folks. This belief has been a cornerstone of Christian faith for centuries. But even if you don't completely agree with Peter, his article invites us to think deeply about our faith and how we live it out. Maybe we can find a middle ground, acknowledging the hope of a future return while also embracing the present reality of the Kingdom of God.

In conclusion, Peter's article is a thought-provoking challenge to traditional Christian eschatology. By suggesting that the Kingdom of God is already here, he calls us to live out our faith actively and responsibly. It's a message that resonates deeply with the inclusive, non-marginalizing teachings of Jesus. So, let's take Peter's insights to heart, roll up our sleeves, and start making the Kingdom of God a reality in our world today. After all, as Jesus said, "The Kingdom of God is in your midst." (Luke 17:20-21)

BRIDGING PERSPECTIVES

8 SOME THOUGHTS ON THE ANTI-DISCRIMINATION DEBATE
BY DR. PETER E. LEWIS PUBLISHED ON: APRIL 8, 2024.

Various groups in society have different ideologies and want the freedom to behave accordingly.

Group 1 is the largest and growing group. It consists of secular, non-religious people who accept divorce, same-sex marriage, etc. In the past they were influenced by Christian values such as caring for the poor, but it remains to be seen if this will continue in the future. With the decline in institutional Christianity this could change, and greed, etc., could dominate as in the pre-Christian Roman empire. Non-religious LGBT+ people are in this group, which does not look kindly on religious intolerance.

Group 2 are religious people who are not LGBT+, divorced, etc. They defend institutional Christianity and tend to take a fundamentalist attitude: that every word in the Bible is truly from God and relevant today. They are afraid that if they surrender on any point, they will lose everything and be expelled.

It is important that religious organizations clearly state how fundamentalist they are. Their schools should make known what their attitude is to being gay, divorced, etc. Then everyone will know where they stand, but the religious authorities might be reluctant to do this because surveys have shown that the school's religious ethos is far down in the list of reasons that parents give for sending their children to these expensive schools, and a large percentage of these parents are in Group 1.

Group 3 are religious people who are LGBT+. They are pressured on both sides. Being religious is considered weird by those in Group 1, and being gay is unacceptable to those who tend to be fundamentalist in Group 2. The task ahead for people in Group 3 and for everyone of good will is to promote the understanding that Christianity still offers a profound way of life and that LGBT+ people are good people who were just born that way. Everyone must make an effort to dispel ignorance and prejudice, because changing the laws would not make any   real   difference.

Source: https://ucforum.unitingchurch.org.au/?p=5528

****

Reflection:

Peter's article, "Some Thoughts on the Anti-Discrimination Debate," dives into the tricky waters of societal divisions over issues like divorce, same-sex marriage, and LGBT+ rights. He splits society into three groups: secular, non-religious folks; religious, non-LGBT+ individuals; and religious LGBT+ individuals. It's a thoughtful breakdown that helps us see just how layered these debates are.

Peter has a propensity for approaching these issues with the same openness and empathy that Jesus did. Remember how Jesus loved shaking things up to help people see each other with more compassion? That's what Peter is aiming for.

Dallas Willard once pointed out that the conservative wing of the Western church often focuses too much on getting people to heaven instead of helping them live heavenly lives here on earth. This means we end up with communities ready for the afterlife but pretty clueless about living fully and lovingly in the present. They might call themselves Christians, but sometimes it feels like they're missing the whole point of being Christ-like.

Take a moment to picture this: you're at a church gathering, and the most radical act of fellowship is sharing a cup of tea and a biscuit. That's it. No deep conversations, no real understanding, just surface-level niceties. For many conservatives, this is the norm, and it's bewildering.

Now, as someone who identifies as queer, I can't help but wonder: what kind of sadistic God would create people one way and then demand they change?

Peter's article brought to mind a cartoon by David Hayward where Jesus is teaching a woman to flip a table, saying, "And then you just flip it like THIS!" It's a perfect metaphor for confronting injustice head-on. Just as Jesus overturned the tables in the temple to challenge corruption, we too should be ready to confront abuse, exploitation, and inequality. This powerful image speaks to the courage needed to stand up against systemic wrongs and advocate for the marginalized.

So, let's break down Peter's three groups:

Group 1: Secular, non-Religious People Peter sees this group as the largest and fastest growing. They've historically been influenced by Christian values, like caring for the poor, but Peter wonders if this will continue as institutional Christianity declines. Without these values, could society become as ruthless as the pre-Christian Roman Empire? It's a valid concern.

Group 2: Religious, non-LGBT+ People This group is all about defending traditional Christianity. They hold onto the belief that every word in the Bible is directly from God and relevant today. They fear that compromising on any point will lead to losing everything. Peter suggests that religious organizations should be upfront about their stances on issues like LGBT+ rights and divorce, even though this might not be what most parents look for when choosing schools for their kids.

Group 3: Religious LGBT+ People These folks face unique pressures, being caught between a secular world that finds their faith strange and a religious world that rejects their identity.

Peter highlights the tough road ahead for them and for all of us: to show that Christianity can still offer a profound way of life and that LGBT+ people are exactly who God made them to be.

Peter's exploration of these issues shines a light on the intersections of identity—race, gender, wealth, sexual orientation—and how they shape our experiences within religious settings.

Peter's article urges a rethinking of how we practice our faith, advocating for a balance between religious freedoms and LGBT+ rights through ongoing dialogue and adaptability. It suggests that churches might need to abandon outdated traditions and embrace diversity and new interpretations to champion social justice and inclusivity. Echoing G.K. Chesterton's insight that "Christianity has died many times and risen again; for it had a God who knew the way out of the grave," the article envisions a transformative renewal of Christianity—a church that truly embodies Jesus' teachings by welcoming and loving without conditions.

HUMBLE RADIANCE

9 WHO IS THE SUFFERING SERVANT IN ISAIAH 53?

By Dr. Peter E. Lewis Published On: May 9, 2024.

This is a plea for Christians to realize the significance of Isaiah 53 for their understanding of who Jesus was and what he did. I believe that he was motivated by love to take on the role of the Suffering Servant in Isaiah 53. This is implied in Paul's statement in his letter to the Galatians, "I live by faith in the Son of God who loved me and gave himself for me." (Gal 2:20b)

But the matter is not as free of dissent as one might think. An important book on the subject is *Jesus and the Suffering Servant: Isaiah 53 and Christian Origins* edited by William Bellinger and William Farmer and published in 1998. In it, Morna Hooker, who was Professor of New Testament at Cambridge University, argued that Isaiah 53 played no significant role in Jesus' understanding of his ministry. She suggested that its use to interpret his ministry began with Paul. Along with several other biblical scholars, she had argued since 1959 that it was the early Church that made the connection between Jesus and Isaiah 53.

More recently, some biblical scholars have regarded Jesus as a peasant who was unable to read Hebrew or Greek. In this case one would have to argue that he knew of Isaiah 53 by hearing it read in Aramaic in the local synagogue. If there was no synagogue at Nazareth, he could easily have walked to another, perhaps even to Capernaum, because he was capable of walking long distances. Nazareth was a small village, but it was only a few kilometres from Sepphoris, which was a centre of Jewish culture. Even if it were more Hellenistic than Jewish at the time, there would have been Jews there who could read Hebrew. Sepphoris was being rebuilt, and a bright young man like Jesus could have taken advantage of these circumstances to learn the Hebrew scriptures.

Although the early Church promoted the idea that Jesus was the Suffering Servant of Isaiah 53, scholars have questioned why the New Testament does not contain quotations of key phrases or sentences from the final verses. The Servant suffers and dies for a reason, and in verses 10, 11 and 12 this is explained. A sentence such as 'The servant will justify many' gives meaning to what Jesus did. The many will be acceptable to God and be with God in his kingdom.

In *Jesus and the Suffering Servant*, David Sapp gives an explanation for the absence of such quotations in the New Testament. He says that there are allusions to verses 10 and 11 but no quotations because the writers of the New Testament (who wrote in Greek) generally quote from the Septuagint, the Greek translation of the Hebrew, but it differs from the Hebrew in the meaning that it gives. It does not include the concept of a sacrificial death. According to Sapp, "The Christian doctrine of atonement rests upon an understanding of Isaiah 53 that is fully present only in the Hebrew versions." The early Christians knew the Hebrew text, but when they "wanted to tell the message of Christ's sacrificial death using *vv. 10-11b*, they could not quote the Greek. They could only allude to the Hebrew." Modern English versions translate the Hebrew, not the Septuagint.

Of course, it was not only Isaiah 53 that influenced Jesus in his teaching and actions but the whole story of Israel's relationship with God as recorded in the Hebrew scriptures. Nevertheless, the writers of the New Testament understood Isaiah 53 to be the divinely ordained pattern for the Messianic mission of Jesus. Three times in Mark's gospel, Jesus says that the Son of Man (meaning himself) must suffer and die, and Paul alludes several times to Jesus' sacrificial death. In 1 Corinthians 15: 3 he writes, "For what I received I passed on to you as of first importance: that Christ died for our sins according to the scriptures." It is difficult to believe that Paul just thought up the connection between Jesus and Isaiah 53 to interpret Jesus' ministry if, as he says in Galatians 1:18, he went to Jerusalem to get acquainted with Peter and stayed with him for fifteen days. During Jesus' ministry, his disciples did not understand his intention. If they had, they might not have followed him to Jerusalem, but after the crucifixion and the resurrection, they understood that he intended to fulfill the role of the Suffering Servant. In 1 Peter 2:21, Peter says, "Christ suffered for you, leaving you an example that you should follow in his steps."

If Jesus did not suffer and die on the cross for me, I cannot see why I should bother to be a Christian, a follower of Jesus Christ. There were and still are many philosophers with wise words on how to live, but if he did, I can say, with Paul, in an existential and emotional way, "Jesus loved *me*, and gave himself for *me*."

In response to what Jesus did for me, I take seriously what he said. He said we should love and forgive, which meant having a self-giving concern for others and oneself. He said in Mark 10:44,45 that his disciples should be the servants of all, "for even the Son of Man came not to be served, but to serve and give his life as a ransom for many." In John 13:15, after washing the feet of his disciples, he said, "I have set you an example that you should do as I have done for you." In other words, they should be like Jesus, and ultimately, this means that they must also take on the role of the Suffering Servant of Isaiah 53 in order to make atonement for the world. So, the answer to the title question is: the Suffering Servant is every Christian, you and me.

Source: https://progressivechristianity.org/resource/who-is-the-suffering-servant-in-isaiah-53/

****

Reflection:

Peter's article on the Suffering Servant in Isaiah 53 extends an invitation to explore how Jesus perceived his mission. Peter believes that Jesus saw himself as the Suffering Servant, motivated by profound love. This perspective aligns beautifully with Paul's words in Galatians

2:20, where Paul speaks of living by faith in the Son of God who loved him and gave himself for him.

I have come to understand that Jesus was the Suffering Servant described in Isaiah 53. This conviction, alongside Peter's, resonates deeply with my understanding. For me, Jesus' role as the Suffering Servant is integral to his mission of love and redemption. It's not just about fulfilling a prophecy but embodying a profound commitment to humanity's salvation. Jesus' sacrificial love, as depicted in Isaiah 53, encapsulates his entire ministry: his healing, teaching, and ultimate sacrifice on the cross.

Peter acknowledges the ongoing scholarly debate surrounding this interpretation. Scholars like Morna Hooker suggest that the early Church, rather than Jesus himself, made the connection between Jesus and Isaiah 53 post-resurrection. This debate enriches our understanding, showing us that there's a tapestry of interpretations rather than a single thread.

Peter also explores the argument about Jesus' literacy. Given that Jesus was a peasant, some argue he might not have been literate in Hebrew or Greek. Peter suggests that Jesus could have absorbed the scriptures by hearing them in Aramaic at the synagogue or through interactions with educated Jews in nearby cities like Sepphoris. This portrayal of Jesus as deeply connected to his cultural and religious environment, even without formal education, is quite compelling. It also reflects the diverse ways knowledge was transmitted in first-century Palestine, emphasizing oral tradition and communal learning over formal literacy.

The discussion about Jesus' literacy is fascinating, as literacy in first-century Palestine was complex. While oral tradition was strong, there were various ways people learned and transmitted religious knowledge.

One intriguing point Peter makes is about the absence of direct quotations from the final verses of Isaiah 53 in the New Testament. He explains that early Christians often used the Septuagint, the Greek translation of Hebrew scriptures, which doesn't emphasize the sacrificial aspect as strongly as the Hebrew text. This might explain why we see allusions rather than direct quotes in the New Testament. Despite this, the themes of suffering and atonement from Isaiah 53 echo throughout the New Testament, especially in Mark's Gospel and

Paul's letters, demonstrating their profound influence on early Christian thought.

Peter concludes by saying that every Christian is called to be a Suffering Servant, following Jesus' example of self-giving love and service. This is a powerful and challenging call to live out our faith in tangible, compassionate ways.

Embracing the role of the Suffering Servant means reflecting the deep love and sacrifice that Jesus embodied. As progressive Christians, we're called to a journey of continuous learning, compassion, and justice. By integrating these inclusive perspectives, we honour the radical and inclusive love Jesus demonstrated. Imagine a world where we are all working to be voices of hope and agents of change—standing alongside the oppressed and marginalized, and striving for a world where love and justice truly prevail.

So, how does this resonate with your own journey and understanding of faith? Are we ready to follow in the footsteps of the Suffering Servant with courage, empathy, and a commitment to justice? Let's keep exploring these ideas together and see how they might reshape our faith and our world.

RAINBOW COMMUNION: FEEDING THE 5,000

10 SPREADING THE GOSPEL

By Dr. Peter E. Lewis Published On: May 30, 2024.

It is important to understand that before every action there is the intention. How people behave depends on their motivation: what drives them to do what they do. For many people it is the connection to family, country, culture, or religion. So, if a person is born into a family in a country where the culture and religion are of a particular kind, that person will act accordingly.

In Australia, I sometimes hear Christians say that their faith is about loving others and trying to do good in the world and not thinking about theology. Of course, this is a reasonable attitude, but what motivates them is not clear: I suspect that for many it is hoping to go to heaven when they die. But the followers of other religions and secular philosophers say much the same. So why is Christianity any different from other religions and from what philosophers say about how people should live their lives?

I believe that at the heart of Christianity there is something special, and it is this unique basic element that should provide the motivation for people to become followers of Jesus of Nazareth. It is his willingness to be the Suffering Servant of God as described by the prophet Isaiah in Chapter 53 of his book. The Servant suffers and dies for a purpose, and Jesus chose to die on the Cross, believing that it would bring in the Kingdom of God. He was motivated by love to pour out his life unto death and bear the sin of many. (Isaiah 53:12; Matthew 26:28,29) Isaiah outlined the divinely ordained pattern for the Messianic mission of Jesus.

Jesus' death on the Cross did bring in the Kingdom because many people today confess that for them Jesus is Lord. (Romans 10:9a) Mark wrote at the end of his gospel that Jesus sits at the right hand of God (Mark 16:19), but he does not rule as earthly rulers do: he rules by love. It is his sacrificial love, his example of self-giving concern for others, that motivates his followers and constitutes the Kingdom. It is what he did as a human being for his fellow human beings: he saved them from a world where Self is king. In that world of darkness (Colossians 1:13) lurk greed, animosity, and all that is evil.

People enter the Kingdom in an existential and emotional way. Christians are with Christ existentially because each human being is an independent conscious entity. The individual understands that Jesus acted out of love for him or her personally, and can say, with St Paul, "Jesus loved me, and gave himself for me." (Galatians 2:20) This existential situation is, I think, a divine construct.

Christians are with Christ emotionally because their response to seeing an innocent man naked and bleeding on the Cross is emotional. They realize that he represents them in a profoundly human way. Emotion or feeling is innate in human nature and an essential part of life. It rouses them to find meaning in what Jesus did on the Cross, and when they realize it was out of love for them, that love penetrates their psyche, and the Holy Spirit enters their heart. (2 Corinthians 1:22)

If Christians want to spread the good news that the Kingdom of God has come they should follow Paul's example and just preach Christ crucified: "I resolved to know nothing while I was with you except Jesus Christ and him crucified." (1 Corinthians 2:2) As Paul said, this is the wisdom of God and the power of God.

Christianity spread rapidly among the Gentiles in the Roman Empire because of the fervent preaching of missionaries like Paul. He emphasized that Christ died for them to enable them to be in the

Kingdom of God and to live in a spiritual way. Human beings need spirituality in their lives, something more than what they experience in the material world. Otherwise, it is like trying to appreciate a painting by analyzing the pigment on the canvas. Paul stressed that being a Christian is a spiritual matter: "Since you have been raised with Christ, set your hearts on things above, where Christ is seated at the right hand of God." (Colossians 3:1)

To revitalize Christianity today, we should focus on what is basic and point to Jesus on the Cross as the ultimate example of self-giving love. Then, we can let the Holy Spirit, who also points to Jesus (John 14:26), transform the world. Being motivated in this way, people will use their God-given talents "to do good in the world." It is the intention that matters, and selfish motivations, such as wanting to get to heaven, are not what Christianity is about.

Source: https://progressivechristianity.org/resource/spreading-the-gospel/

****

Reflection:

Peter's article, "Spreading the Gospel," has some good ideas about Christian motivations and the essence of faith. He begins by reminding us that our actions stem from our intentions. It's a reminder that what drives us to act is deeply founded in what we hold dear, whether it's family, culture, or faith. In Australia, Peter observes that many Christians focus on loving others and doing good, but sometimes their deeper motivations aren't fully articulated. He suggests that for many, it might be the hope of reaching heaven.

So, as we ponder these reflections, remember: while aiming for heaven, it's a good idea to make sure we're not stumbling over earthly obstacles along the way. After all, it's hard to spread the Gospel effectively if you're tripping over your own shoelaces!

Peter believes that what sets Christianity apart is something unique and beautiful: Jesus' role as the Suffering Servant from Isaiah 53. This is not just about fulfilling a prophecy; it's about embodying a profound commitment to humanity's salvation. Jesus' sacrificial love, choosing to die on the cross to bring about the Kingdom of God, defines Christianity. His willingness to suffer and die out of love is a powerful testament to the essence of our faith. This act of self-giving love, more than anything else, motivates Christians to follow him.

Peter also touches on the profound emotional and existential connection that Christians feel with Jesus. Seeing Jesus' sacrifice on the cross evokes a deep emotional response, making his love and sacrifice personal and real for believers. This emotional connection is essential in spreading the Gospel because it resonates deeply with people on a human level. It's about realizing that Jesus' love is not just for humanity in general, but for each of us individually.

Peter's call to focus on the basics of Christianity—pointing to Jesus on the cross as the ultimate example of self-giving love—is both simple and profound. By preaching Christ crucified, as Paul did, and allowing the Holy Spirit to work, we can transform the world. This focus on selfless love and service, rather than selfish motivations like wanting to get to heaven, is the true essence of Christianity.

In embracing this perspective, we can enrich Peter's argument by incorporating other theologies. Such perspectives could highlight Jesus' solidarity with the oppressed and challenge systems of injustice, offering a more inclusive understanding of his mission. By doing so, we honour the inclusive and radical love that Jesus demonstrated.

So, what do you think? How does this understanding of Jesus' sacrificial love and the call to self-giving service resonate with your own journey and faith? Let's continue this uplifting conversation and explore how we can live out these profound truths in our everyday lives, reflecting Jesus' love, justice, and compassion in everything we do.

EPIPHANY AT THE CROSS

11 THE CROSS: A PERSONAL REFLECTION

BY DR. PETER E. LEWIS PUBLISHED ON: JULY, 2024.

I confess that until a few years ago I was a 'know-all'. I had been a Christian all my life and had obtained an honours degree in divinity from London University. I knew everything about church history and theology, and I could even read Hebrew and the New Testament in Greek. But what happened at church one day changed my thinking entirely.

On that day I attended a prayer meeting with some of the parishioners, and I happened to sit next to a little old lady. As you know, the Anglican church and other similar churches abound in little old ladies. Although this particular little old lady had always attended church on Sunday and was involved in the life of the church, I had never taken any notice of what she said. After all, she was just a little old lady, and I knew everything.

When the time came to pray, each of us said something. The little old lady had a soft voice, but I heard her prayer. She spoke to Jesus and said, "Thank you for what you did for me on the Cross."

I immediately thought, "This is ridiculous. How could the suffering and death of Jesus of Nazareth two thousand years ago have anything to do with this little old lady? It was just foolishness." Then I remembered what St Paul had written in his letter to the Galatians, "I live by faith in the Son of God who loved me and gave himself for me." He was saying what the little old lady had said. They resonated with each other, and I realized that the great saint himself could have been sitting next to me.

The little old lady and Paul were speaking as individuals before God, and to understand what they were saying, one has to acknowledge the great Mystery. It is everyone's existential experience of life: the phenomenon of the individuality of consciousness. In the simplest terms it is "Why am I me?" In a profound way, although we seem to be incorporated in a material world, we are completely on our own before God, and what God in Christ did on the Cross applies directly to each one of us. I now understand and can say, "Jesus loved *me* and gave himself for *me*." (Galatians 2:20)

Why is the death of Jesus of Nazareth so vital? Many good men have suffered and died unfairly in the past. On the face of it he was just a 'loser', another battler crushed by the wheel of fate. Did his suffering and death have any purpose? What meaning could it have? Why did he go to Jerusalem and provoke the authorities as he did?

As St Paul said, Jesus gave himself. He was not a passive pawn in the process. He deliberately chose to suffer and die for a reason, and I believe that reason is to be found in the Old Testament. He was motivated by love for his fellow human beings to take on the role of the Suffering Servant in Isaiah 53. The little old lady and everyone who lives by faith in the Son of God are included in that existential and sacrificial love.

The prophet Isaiah had predicted that there would be a man who would suffer and die in obedience to God's will (Isaiah 53:10a, Cf. Mark 14:36) and in so doing, "justify many" (Isaiah 53:11b). To justify many, meant to make them acceptable to God, to be with God in his kingdom. Because Jesus suffered and died on the Cross, the little old lady is in God's kingdom and has God's spirit in her heart. Isaiah described for Jesus the divinely ordained path to follow in order to make atonement for the world.

But that is not all. Isaiah said that after the suffering of his soul the Servant would see the light of life. (Isaiah 53:11a) This has been interpreted to mean that he would be resurrected. I believe that Jesus did come alive again and that his Resurrection confirmed all that Isaiah had written. By fulfilling the role of the Suffering Servant (Cf. Luke 18:31) Jesus becomes the risen triumphant Christ. Love overcomes everything.

Source: Supplied

****

Reflection:

Peter's article, "The Cross: A Personal Reflection," is a touching and insightful exploration of his spiritual journey, filled with relatable moments and deep theological insights. Let's walk through it together in an engaging way.

Peter starts by sharing a personal confession: he once thought he knew it all. With an honours degree in divinity and the ability to read Hebrew and Greek, Peter was confident in his understanding of theology. However, a simple encounter at a prayer meeting with a little old lady turned his perspective upside down.

Picture this: Peter, a learned theologian, attends a prayer meeting and sits next to a woman who, to him, seemed quite ordinary. When it was her turn to pray, she thanked Jesus for what he did for her on the Cross. Peter found this surprising. How could an event from two thousand years ago impact her life today? Then, he remembered Paul's words from Galatians 2:20, "I live by faith in the Son of God who loved me and gave himself for me." This realization hit Peter like a bolt of lightning. The woman and Paul were expressing the same truth: Jesus' sacrifice on the Cross was deeply personal and profound for each believer.

Peter beautifully illustrates how this moment led him to a deeper understanding of individuality and consciousness. He reflects on the existential question, "Why am I me?" Despite being part of a material world, each person stands alone before God, and Jesus' act on the Cross applies directly to every individual. This insight is both profound and accessible, making us see Jesus' sacrificial love in a new light.

Peter then connects this to Isaiah 53, explaining how Jesus took on the role of the Suffering Servant. This connection helps us understand that Jesus' death wasn't just the fate of a "loser" but a deliberate act of love. The little old lady's faith, Peter's newfound understanding, and the prophecy from Isaiah all come together to show how each believer is enveloped in this existential and sacrificial love.

In the final part of his reflection, Peter talks about the Resurrection, emphasizing that Jesus' rising from the dead confirms everything Isaiah had written. This triumphant resurrection is the ultimate victory of love over all. It's a powerful reminder that love, indeed, overcomes everything.

Peter's reflection is a beautifully written account of a personal spiritual awakening. It highlights the profound and personal nature of Jesus' sacrifice, encouraging us to see the Cross not just as a historical event but as a living, transformative reality in our own lives.

For us, as progressive Christians, Peter's journey resonates deeply. It reminds us to embrace the inclusive and radical love that Jesus demonstrated. This love challenges us to live out our faith in ways that stand in solidarity with the oppressed and marginalized, reflecting the same sacrificial love that Jesus showed.

What do you think? How does Peter's reflection on the Cross and the Suffering Servant speak to your own spiritual journey?

RADIANT GRACE

12 ORIGINAL SIN

By Dr. Peter E. Lewis Published On: July 2024

I believe in God and an original blessing, which is the gift of life in a beautiful world, but with that blessing human beings were allowed to have free will so that God and His (or Her) divine love could be freely responded to and not in any way forced or controlled. I understand original sin to be the tendency of all human beings to turn away from God towards Self, and what Jesus (and God) did on the cross enabled God to accept human beings just as they are when they turn to Him in faith and love. As the prophet said, "He bore the sin of many." (Isaiah 53:12. Cf. Mt 26:28) What Jesus did on the cross overcomes original sin and everything that separates us from God, even death.

The crucifixion is the central point in the Christian story, but it makes no sense unless it is explained by his followers that Jesus believed that his suffering had a purpose, that he would save many people. This is emphasized by St Paul and the gospel writers (e.g. Mark 10:45) and it gives the whole crucifixion scene the power of love. Otherwise, there is no reason for anybody to respond to this divine drama.

Jesus was not forced to take up the cross: he assented to God's plan for humanity. Motivated by love, he willingly took on the role of the Suffering Servant as described in Isaiah 53. As the human expression of God, Jesus on the cross shows God in complete weakness, except for the power of love.

Jesus gave himself, and this self-giving way of thinking or emotion is at the heart of what is meant by love in the New Testament. The crucifixion represents this sacrificial love in its ultimate form, and human beings were created with an awareness of this ultimate love. What mother or father would not give their life to save a child, and what husband or wife would not give their life to save the other? The original goodness of human beings is a fact of life. This is not the same as saying that salvation can be gained through works: it refers to an awareness, a potential element in human nature. Each human being can choose to activate this gift of God, turn towards Him and be in a personal loving relationship with Him. It is the key to heaven.

Unfortunately, some theologians considered human sexuality to be sinful and its products, human beings, to be unacceptable to God because of this stain that they called original sin. They thought that the stain made human beings quite separate from God and devoid of any ability to relate to Him. But once it is understood that there is essentially nothing wrong with human sexuality, this idea of original sin can be rejected.

Although God created human beings with free will and the tendency to turn to Self, He also gave them the capacity to love as Jesus loved. This God-given element in human nature resonates with the divine love shown by Jesus on the cross. It is like a spark that can flare up into a flame when activated by faith and love. It is God's grace, the undeserved gift to every human being, and the flame is the Holy Spirit. God lets human beings do whatever they want, but in each one He puts a pinch of holiness.

Source: https://progressivechristianity.org/resource/original-sin/

****

Reflection:

Peter's article on "Original Sin" is like a breath of fresh air in theological discussions. He starts by flipping the traditional concept on its head, introducing the idea of an "original blessing." This is such an uplifting way to begin, reminding us that life itself is a gift, and it's filled with opportunities for love and connection.

Peter dives into free will, which he says allows us to respond to God's love genuinely and freely. This is a comforting thought – that our relationship with God is based on mutual love and respect, not on control or coercion.

His explanation of original sin is straightforward and relatable. Peter describes it as our tendency to turn away from God and focus on ourselves. It's a struggle we can all understand. He then highlights the power of Jesus' sacrifice, which allows God to accept us as we are, provided we turn to Him in faith and love. This is a message of hope and transformation.

Peter's take on the crucifixion is particularly moving. He emphasizes that Jesus' suffering had a purpose – to save many people, as emphasized by St. Paul and the gospel writers. This gives the crucifixion scene its incredible power of love. Without this context, it could seem like just another tragic event. But Peter beautifully articulates how it represents the ultimate act of sacrificial love.

He talks about Jesus' self-giving love, which is central to New Testament teachings. Peter's analogy about parents sacrificing themselves for their children is touching and relatable. It underscores the inherent goodness and potential for love within humanity, aligning with progressive theology that emphasizes the worth and dignity of every person.

Peter also challenges the notion that human sexuality is inherently sinful. He argues that there is nothing wrong with human sexuality, thus rejecting the traditional idea of original sin as a stain. This is a liberating perspective, resonating with liberation and feminist theologies, which emphasize that our bodies and sexuality are good and holy parts of who we are.

His description of God's grace as a spark that can ignite into a flame of the Holy Spirit is poetic and inspiring. It reminds us that we all carry a piece of the divine within us, and through faith and love, this divine spark can become a guiding light in our lives.

In summary, Peter's article is a heartfelt and theologically rich reflection on original sin, grace, and love. It challenges us to see the divine potential within ourselves and others and to live out our faith in ways that are both profound and practical. It's a beautiful call to embrace the original blessing of life and to respond to God's love with our own acts of love and kindness.

As this is the last critique, it's fitting to end with a profound reminder: We are not bound by the chains of sin but are invited into a relationship of grace and love with the divine. This relationship calls us to see each person as a bearer of God's image, worthy of love and dignity. Remember the thief on the cross beside Jesus?

In his final moments, he simply asked to be remembered, and Jesus assured him, "Today you will be with me in paradise" (Luke 23:43). This powerful encounter highlights that our journey of faith isn't about attaining perfection or theological advancement, but about growing in love and grace, responding to the divine spark within us, and sharing that light with the world. By embracing this truth, we can transform our world, one act of love at a time. This is the heart of the gospel and the essence of our Christian calling. Indeed, "today you will be with me in paradise."

EUCHARISTIC JOY

13 MY FAITH

It might be helpful to some people if I briefly describe my Christian faith, which is a simple one. It is based on the Bible but not in a fundamentalist way. In fact, I think some parts of the Bible are just plain wrong. For example, if God told Abraham to kill his son, then he is evil and not a god I could worship. Similarly, I cannot accept that Jesus was sacrificed to appease a god who was angry with sinful humans, as animals were sacrificed in the Temple in Jerusalem. My faith is focused on the historical Jesus, what he said and did, and I believe he was motivated by love. In Greek, this love is αγαπη (agape), which essentially means a self-giving concern for others. Jesus was not a passive character, but the active agent in the process that enabled communion between human beings and God, who is at the heart of the great Mystery in which we exist. God for me is the Creator and the source of my life, and therefore something positive and good. As the source of life, God must be "the living God." (Hebrews 10:31)

I take an existential view of Jesus: he loved *me* and gave himself for *me*. Therefore, I too must be concerned for the world and everything

60

and everybody in it in an unselfish way. In other words, I must try to love   like   Jesus.

If Jesus was motivated by love to bring human beings and God together, how did he do it? I believe the answer is the Suffering Servant as described by the prophet Isaiah, especially Isaiah 52:13 to 53:12, and in some of the psalms. Jesus took on the role of the Servant believing that it would bring in the Kingdom of God, and it did. As St Paul said in   Colossians   1:13,   we   are   in   the   Kingdom.

The key question in theology is why was Jesus in Jerusalem behaving in such a provocative way? Was he just protesting, was he there to initiate an uprising of the people, or was he fulfilling the role of the Servant in Isaiah 53? If he was the Servant, then he was provoking the authorities to kill him. I believe with the early church that the Servant figure of Isaiah was the "divinely ordained pattern for the Messianic mission of Jesus." (New Bible Dictionary, page 1094) Jesus provided the example of self-giving concern for others that the world needed, and God ordained. Following Jesus means overcoming selfishness, pride, greed, animosity, and everything that is evil in the world.

For me, what clinches this understanding of Jesus is the Last Supper. Out of love, he gives himself in the bread and wine. He pours out his life (Mark 14:24) as the Servant poured out his life (Isaiah 53:12). In   this   way   his   spirit   lives   in   me.

My faith is human-oriented, although I do not deny that Jesus was divinely inspired, that he was both human and divine. My theology might   be   simple,   but   it   works   for   me.

ABOUT THE AUTHOR

Peter Lewis is an independent Australian scholar not connected to any university or seminary. Although he has postgraduate qualifications in biblical studies, his career has been medical. He is a fellow of the Royal College of Surgeons of England and has worked as a surgeon in developing countries (Bangladesh and the Solomon Islands).

Upon returning to Australia, he served as the vice-president of Hopewell Hospice Services on the Gold Coast for twenty years. Peter is also a numismatist and has written books and many articles about coins relating to the history of Christianity. Currently, he is a Research Associate for the Centre for Coins, Culture and Religious History at cccrh.org.

ABOUT THE EDITOR

Shane holds a Graduate Diploma in Theology from St. Francis Theological College, University of Divinity, Australia, and pursued further studies in Christian Leadership at Christ Church, University of Oxford in 2023. As a published author and editor of TheGoodNewsBlog.org, he envisions a world where everyone is celebrated, and where the church fully embraces the radical spirit of Jesus' teachings. His website, which reaches tens of thousands monthly, offers progressive resources that welcome newcomers, heal church-related wounds, enrich faith, and empower leaders, amplifying voices like Peter's.

BIBLIOGRAPHY

Althaus-Reid, M. (2007). *The Queer God*. Routledge.

Bellinger, W. H., & Farmer, W. R. (2009). *Jesus and the suffering servant: Isaiah 53 and Christian origins*. Wipf & Stock.

Centre for coins, culture and Religious History Foundation. Centre for Coins, Culture and Religious History Foundation. (n.d.). https://cccrh.org/

Cheng, P. S. (2024). *Radical love: Introduction to queer theology*. CHURCH PUBLISHING INC.

Chesterton, G. K. (n.d.). *The Five Deaths of the Faith*. G.K. CHESTERTON: THE EVERLASTING MAN. https://www.worldinvisible.com/library/chesterton/everlasting/part2c6.htm

Guest, D., & Jacobson, J. (2019). *The queer bible commentary edited by Deryn Guest*. MTM.

Hayward, D. (2021, April 15). *A commissioned piece: Learning to flip tables with Jesus*. Nakedpastor. https://nakedpastor.com/blogs/news/table-flipping-master-class

Home: ISCAST – Christianity and science in conversation. ISCAST. (2024, August 30). https://iscast.org/

Infancy gospel of James. Infancy Gospel of James, or Protevangelium (Roberts-Donaldson translation). (n.d.). https://www.earlychristianwritings.com/text/infancyjames-roberts.html

Lewis, C. S. (1970). *God in the dock*. William B. Eerdmans Publishing Co.

Lewis, P. E. (n.d.). *Peter Lewis*. Anglican focus. https://anglicanfocus.org.au/contributors/peter-lewis/

Lewis, P. E. (1993). *Susan's faith: A theological novel*. Happiness Books.

Lewis, P. E. (2020). *The ending of mark's gospel: The key to understanding the gospels and Christianity*. Zeus Publications.

LGBT | English meaning - Cambridge dictionary. (n.d.-a). https://dictionary.cambridge.org/dictionary/english/lgbt

Midjourney. (n.d.-b). https://www.midjourney.com/home/

Mulherin, D. C. (n.d.). *Science and Christianity: Understanding the Conflict Myth*. Garratt Publishing.

New Bible dictionary. (1996). *New bible dictionary*. Intervarsity Press.

Open discussion on Progressive Christianity | Open Dialogue and inclusive action in the Uniting Church in Australia, and with

Friends of the UCA. in our 24th year. (n.d.-c).

https://ucforum.unitingchurch.org.au/

Parker, D. C. (2009). *Codex Bezae*. Cambridge University Press.

Progressivechristianity.org home. ProgressiveChristianity.org. (2024, May

21). https://progressivechristianity.org/

Reynolds, S. S. (2023). *Faith & sexuality reconciling LGBT+ people and*

Christianity. Reynolds, Shane St. LifeRich Publishing.

Spong, J. S. (2014). *Liberating the gospels: Reading the Bible with Jewish eyes*.

HarperCollins e-Books.

St Michaels Exploring Belonging. (n.d.-d).

https://stmichaels.org.au/wp-content/uploads/2022/09/St-

Michaels-Day-2022-online.pdf

TheGoodNewsBlog.org - Progressive Christianity. (n.d.).

https://www.thegoodnewsblog.org/

Visio divina. Seaforth Anglican. (n.d.).

https://www.seaforthanglican.org.au/visio-divina

Willard, D. (2021). *Renovation of the heart: Putting on the character of Christ*.

NavPress.

Printed in Great Britain
by Amazon

47779797R00053